From Your Friends At The MAILBOX®

NOVEMBER

A MONTH OF REPRODUCIBLES AT YOUR FINGERTIPS!

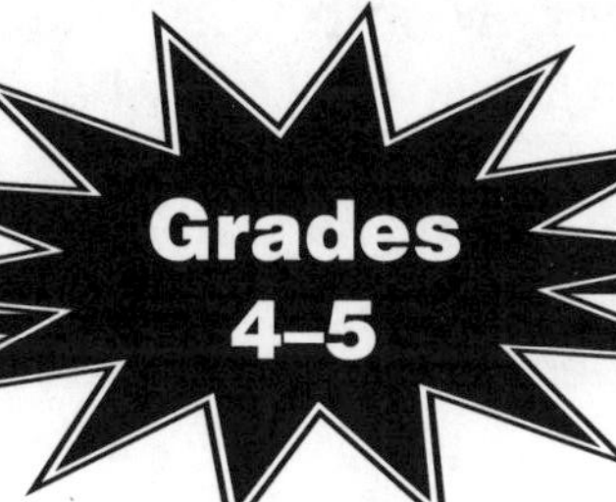

Senior Editor:
Thad H. McLaurin

Associate Editor:
Cindy Mondello

Writers:
Julie Alarie, Marcia Barton, Therese Durhman, Rusty Fischer, Thad H. McLaurin, Cindy Mondello, Gail Peckumn, Patricia Twohey

Art Coordinator:
Clevell Harris

Artists:
Teresa Davidson, Nick Greenwood, Clevell Harris, Sheila Krill, Barry Slate, Donna K. Teal

Cover Artist:
Jennifer Tipton Bennett

ISBN #1-56234-254-1

Manufactured in the United States

10 9 8 7 6 5 4 3 2 1

Table Of Contents

Name ____________________

November Free Time

MONDAY	TUESDAY	WEDNESDAY	THURSDAY	FRIDAY
November 1 is National Author's Day. Recommend a book by your favorite author to a friend.	The first full week of November is Cat Week. Explain why you think a cat is said to have nine lives.	Describe your family's favorite Thanksgiving traditions or a new tradition you'd like to start.	In 1837, Illinois housewives protested against the high prices of butter ($.08 a pound) and eggs ($.06 a dozen). Compare today's egg and butter prices with those of 1837.	On November 5, 1924, the first crossword-puzzle book was published. Create your own crossword puzzle using words from this week's spelling list.
Garrett Morgan, a Black American inventor, patented the traffic light in November 1923. What would life be like today if the traffic light had never been invented?	Use each letter in Thanksgiving to spell something for which you are thankful. T urkey H appiness A unt Beverly N ana K indness S G I V I N G	Milton Bradley, an American games manufacturer, was born on November 8, 1836. What is your favorite board game? Is it made by Milton Bradley's company? BATTL Game Of LIFE ™	Mom Dad Billy List the names of people you are thankful to have in your life.	On November 10, 1903, Mary Anderson patented the windshield wiper. Make a list of ten other simple inventions that make your life much safer and easier.
Write a thank-you note to someone who has recently been kind or helpful to you. Thank You	Jules Leotard introduced the flying trapeze at a circus in Paris in November 1859. Illustrate your favorite circus act.	Illustrate and describe the most unusual snack food you've ever eaten. PEANUT BUTTER	Walt Disney's movie *Fantasia* premiered in New York on November 13, 1940. Who is your favorite Disney character? Why?	November 17 is Homemade Bread Day. In honor of this day, make up a name and design a logo for a brand-new bakery. Billy's Bread
Do your classmates prefer a particular brand of jeans? Take a poll to find out. Survey each student; then graph your data.	The longest banana split ever made (over one mile long) was created in Australia on November 20, 1976. Illustrate your favorite dessert and list its ingredients.	Nominate a book for the next Newbery Award. Write the title of the book, the author's name, and a brief explanation telling why it should win the award. And the winner is...	Give turkeys a break! Create an unusual Thanksgiving meal. ?	In 1842, the first volcanic eruption recorded in the United States occurred at Mount Lassen in California. Describe this event as if you had been an eyewitness.

 Note To The Teacher: Have each student staple a copy of this page in a file folder. Direct students to store their completed work inside their folders.

NOVEMBER
Events And Activities For The Family

Directions: Select at least one activity below to complete as a family by the end of November. *(Challenge: See if your family can complete all three activities.)*

Be A Weather Forecaster

The U.S. Weather Bureau made its first weather observation on November 1, 1870. In honor of this occasion, sit down with your family and watch a local weather forecast on television. Based on what the meteorologist has to say, have each family member fill out a "Prediction Page." On a sheet of notebook paper, have each family member write his or her predictions for the next day's forecast, such as the exact high temperature, exact low temperature, and amount of rain. The next day, compare your predictions with the weather page from your local newspaper to see which family member was right. Let the winner decide what's for dessert that night!

I am thankful for my dog Brutus...

National Family Week

National Family Week is observed the week of Thanksgiving. To celebrate, start a new family tradition in your house. During the week, interview all of the family members who will be attending Thanksgiving dinner at your home. Ask each guest what he or she is thankful for and write down each answer. Leaving out any names, copy each answer onto a separate unlined sheet of paper. Illustrate each answer with crayons or markers; then roll each answer and illustration into a scroll and tie it with a piece of fall-colored yarn. Place one scroll on each guest's dinner plate. Before eating, have each guest open his or her scroll one at a time and read it out loud. See if your family can guess whose answer is on each scroll. Once the answer is revealed, let its owner keep the scroll as a holiday souvenir he or she will always be thankful for!

Children's Book Week

The third full week of November is designated as Children's Book Week. Take advantage of this opportunity by taking your family to visit the local library. In the children's section, select a book the whole family will enjoy reading. Each night of the week, spend time together as a family reading out loud from the book you've chosen. Rotate family members each night so that everyone gets a chance to read. Celebrate Children's Book Week every week by making family reading time a new tradition in your house.

Note To The Teacher: Give one copy of this page to each student at the beginning of the month. Encourage each family to complete at least one activity by the end of November.

National Author's Day

Observed on November 1 since 1929, National Author's Day is set aside as a day to celebrate the contributions of American authors by writing letters to favorite authors and flying American flags.

Authors from A to Z

Avi doesn't tell his real name.
Books are special to Avi—he was once a librarian.
Charlotte Doyle finds adventure on the ocean.
Dyslexia is something Avi deals with when he's writing.
Emily is Avi's twin's name.
Fighting Ground is a book about 24 hours of Jonathan's life.

Authors A To Z

Encourage your students to show they know their favorite author from *A* to *Z* with this fun research project. Allow each reader in your class to choose an author to research. The student should have read two or more of that author's stories or books before beginning to research interesting facts about the author's life, education, and sources for stories. After all the research is complete, challenge each student to create a one- or two-page "Author's Alphabet," writing one fact about the author or her books for each letter of the alphabet. Collect the decorated final drafts in a binder to keep near the classroom library as a quick preview of authors and their works that your students can use when they're looking for a good book.

Pseudonym Sleuths

Some authors choose to use a *pseudonym,* or *pen name,* when they write. A *pseudonym* is simply a fictitious name that an author uses to disguise his real name. Turn your students into private eyes by having them search through dictionaries, encyclopedias, and other resources to find out the identities of the incognito authors listed on page 6. During the search, challenge your students to come up with other authors who use a *nom de plume* (pen name). Keep a running list of authors and their pen names as students discover them throughout the year. To encourage writing in your classroom, have each student select a pen name for himself. Only you will know each pen name's true identity. Periodically have students write under their pen names. Post the writings for everyone to enjoy reading.

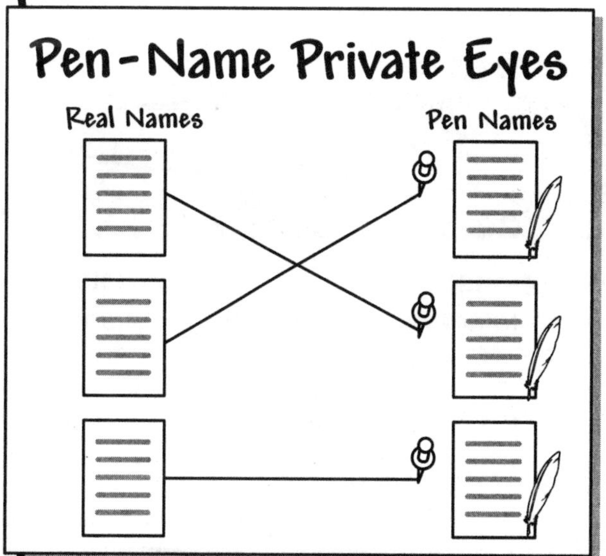

Pen-Name Private Eyes

Real Names | Pen Names

Name ____

Pen-Name Private Eyes

Did you know that some authors use a *pseudonym,* or *pen name,* when they write? In fact, some authors use more than one! A *pseudonym* is a fictitious name that an author uses to disguise his real name.

Directions: Crack the case of the *incognito* (disguised) authors by matching each author's real name to his or her pen name(s). Use reference books to help you as you play pen-name private eye!

Authors' Real Names

____ 1. Louisa May Alcott, author of *Little Women*
____ 2. Hans Christian Andersen, author of fairy tales
____ 3. Isaac Asimov, science-fiction writer
____ 4. Charles Dodgson
____ 5. Theodor Seuss Geisel
____ 6. Edgar Rice Burroughs, author of *Tarzan* books
____ 7. Charles Dickens, author of *A Christmas Carol*
____ 8. L. Frank Baum, author of *The Wonderful Wizard Of Oz*
____ 9. James Fenimore Cooper, author of *The Last Of The Mohicans*
____ 10. Joan Aiken, author of *The Wolves Of Willoughby Chase*

Authors' Pen Names

a. Dr. A, Paul French

b. Lewis Carroll, author of *Alice's Adventures In Wonderland*

c. Norman Bean, Craig Shaw Gardner

d. Boz, Timothy Sparks

e. A. M. Barnard

f. Villiam Christian Walter

g. Jane Morgan

h. Theo Lesieg, Dr. Seuss, author of *The Cat In The Hat* and others

i. Nicholas Dee, Rosie Lee

j. John Estes Cook, Edith Van Dyne

Directions: Write each underlined letter found in the pen-name list above in the correct blanks below to answer the following question: What is another word for a pen name?

__ __ __   __ __   __ __ __ __ __

f d c   e j   a b h g i

Bonus Box: On the back of this sheet, list three reasons why an author might choose not to use his or her real name. After seeing these authors' pen names, how do you think an author chooses a pseudonym to use?

 Note To The Teacher: Use with "Pseudonym Sleuths" on page 5.

Name ______________________________________

A Prince (Or Princess) Of An Idea!

Children's writer Madeleine L'Engle, author of *A Wrinkle In Time,* calls writing an "essential function, like sleeping and breathing." She has a real writer's habit: she writes every single day.

Directions: To be as dedicated to writing as Madeleine L'Engle, you must always be on the lookout for things to write *about*. List below several story ideas. These do not have to be detailed; a simple word or phrase will do. Just jot down something that will make you remember the topic you want to write about. Keep this list handy and add to it anytime a new writing idea pops into your mind. During your spare time or journal-writing time, choose a topic to write about. You never can tell when you have a real prince (or princess) of an idea on your hands!

Writing Ideas

1. ______________________
2. ______________________
3. ______________________
4. ______________________
5. ______________________
6. ______________________
7. ______________________
8. ______________________
9. ______________________
10. ______________________
11. ______________________
12. ______________________
13. ______________________
14. ______________________
15. ______________________
16. ______________________
17. ______________________
18. ______________________
19. ______________________
20. ______________________
21. ______________________
22. ______________________
23. ______________________
24. ______________________

Note To The Teacher: Duplicate one copy of this page for each student.

Name ____________________

Write Your Favorite Author

The idea for National Author's Day came about when a woman named Nellie McPherson wrote to her favorite author telling him how much she liked a story he had written. In reply, he sent her an autographed copy of another story. She was so pleased that she started a campaign to set aside a day each year to remind people to write to their favorite authors.

Directions: In the space below, write a letter to your favorite author telling him your opinion of your favorite book. Also ask questions about his writing process, such as where he gets his ideas or what he does first when beginning a new novel. Proofread your letter carefully; then mail it and wait for a response.

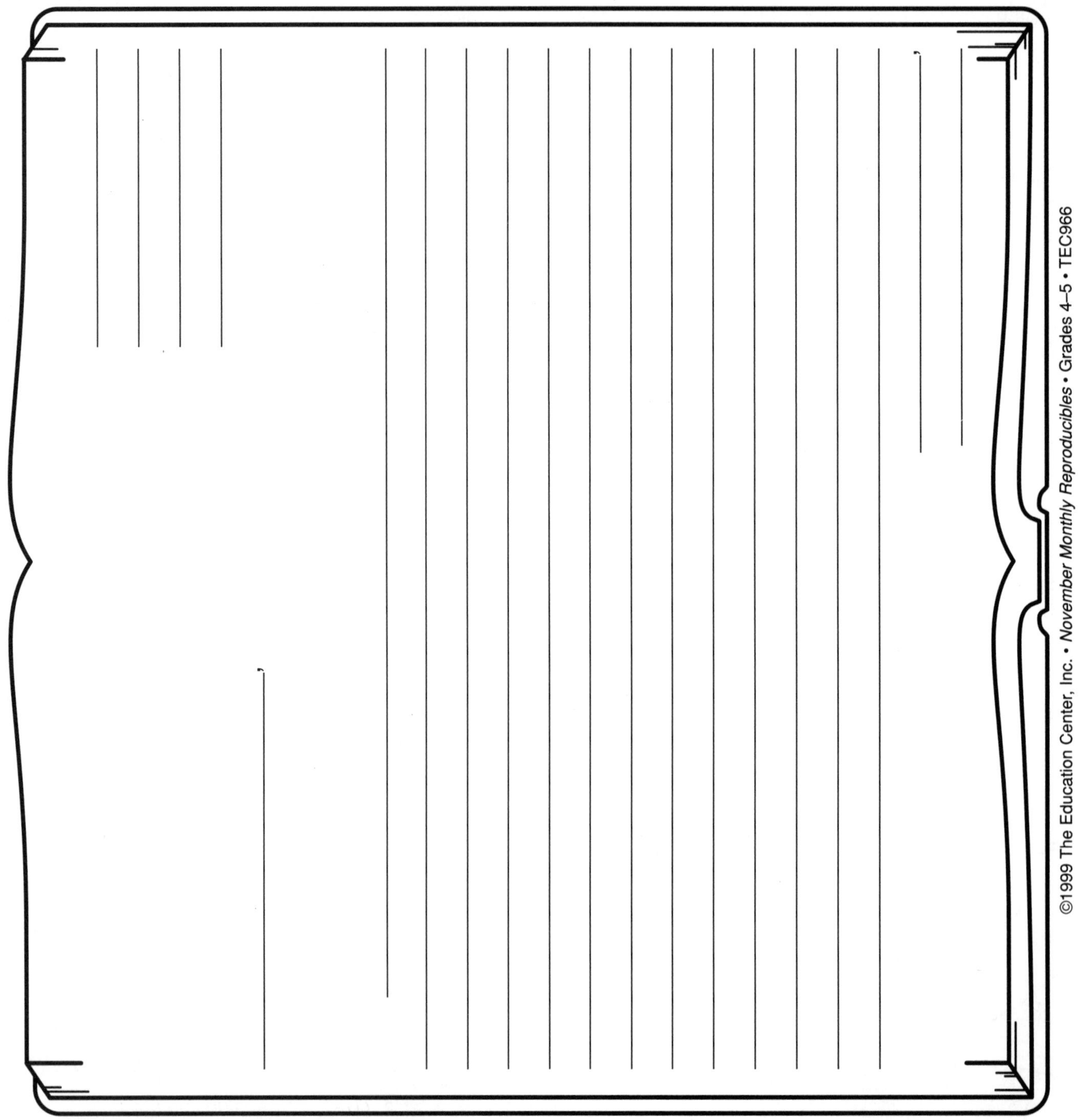

Note To The Teacher: Duplicate one copy of this page for each student. Have each student send his letter to the publisher of his favorite author's book.

Aviation History Month

Aviation History Month is observed in November because it is the anniversary of the aeronautical experiments conducted by Joseph and Etienne Montgolfier. These two brothers lived in France in 1782 and experimented with filling paper and fabric bags with smoke and hot air. Their experiments led to the invention of the hot-air balloon, the first airplane flight, and the science of aviation and flight. Celebrate these incredible accomplishments by sharing these activities with your students.

An Uplifting Experience

Encourage your students to discover the principle of *lift* to help them better understand airplane aerodynamics with these activities. Set up the following seven simple stations. The directions for each station are listed on page 10. *(The outcome of each station is in parentheses at the end of each station's set-up directions below.)* Then divide students into seven groups. Give each group one copy of page 10. Assign each group to a different station. Set a timer for five minutes. Instruct each group to complete the activity and record the results on the reproducible. When the timer sounds, have each group rotate to the next numbered station. After each group has completed each station, follow up with a discussion of how lift works in airplanes. *(Because of the shape of airplane wings, air travels faster over the curved tops of the wings. This faster moving air creates an area of low pressure. This is an application of Bernoulli's principle. It is this difference in air pressure above and beneath the wing that causes the wing to lift. In each of the station activities, moving air was creating an area of less pressure, so objects moved in the direction of the moving air, not away from it.)*

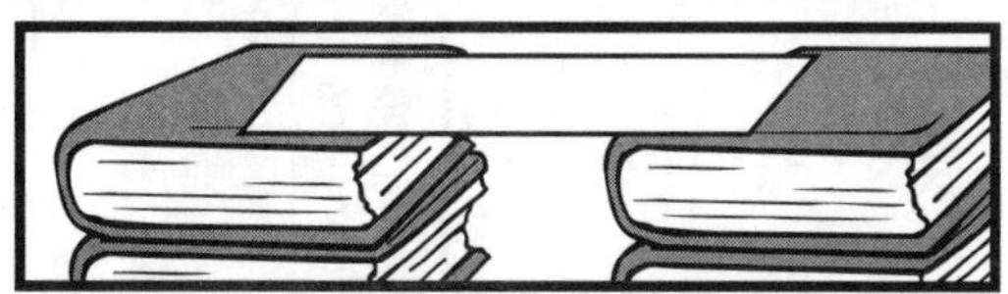

Station 1: Place four same-sized books in two equal stacks several inches apart on a table with a sheet of notebook paper resting on top as shown. *(The paper bends down instead of up.)*

Station 2: Place a small funnel and a Ping-Pong® ball on a table. *(The Ping-Pong® ball will stay in the funnel as long as they keep blowing hard—which isn't very long.)*

Station 3: Tie a 12-inch length of string to the stem of each of two apples. Hang the apples about 1 1/2 inches apart and the same distance above a table. *(The apples come together and touch when air is blown between them.)*

Station 4: Set out a 20-ounce plastic bottle and a small piece of crumpled paper (smaller than the opening of the bottle). *(The paper will pop out of the bottle instead of going into the bottle.)*

Station 5: Set out a small plastic (lightweight) counting chip on a desk or table. *(The chip goes up into the air.)*

Station 6: Set out several 3" x 5" strips of newsprint or notebook paper. *(The paper strip lifts up.)*

Station 7: Set out two sheets of typing or notebook paper. *(The two sheets come together and touch.)*

Names ______________________

Air Power

Directions: First, read the directions for each station. Second, write your prediction about what will happen at the station. Third, complete the activity. Fourth, write a brief summary of the results. Use your results to answer the questions below the chart.

Station	Prediction	Results
#1. Position yourself at eye level with the paper on top of the books. Blow under the paper. What happens to the paper?		
#2. Turn the funnel upside down and hold the Ping-Pong® ball inside the funnel with your index finger. Blow as hard as you can for as long as you can through the narrow opening. Remove your finger as you continue to blow. What happens to the ball?		
#3. Blow hard in the space between the apples. What happens to the apples?		
#4. Lay the plastic bottle on its side. Place the crumpled piece of paper inside the opening of the bottle. Blow across the opening (sideways) of the bottle. What happens to the paper? Then turn the bottle towards you, put the paper wad back in the opening, and blow straight at the paper. What happens to the paper?		
#5. Place the plastic chip close to the edge of the desk. Position your mouth level with the chip, then blow hard across the top of the chip. What happens to the chip?		
#6. Hold a strip of newsprint or notebook paper in front of your face right underneath your bottom lip and blow across the top of the paper. What happens to the paper?		
#7. Hold one sheet of paper in each hand about two inches apart and blow between the sheets of paper. What happens to the paper?		

1. How were your predictions different from the actual results? ______________________
2. In what way(s) were all of these experiments alike? ______________________
3. Does moving air or still air create an area of high pressure? ______________________
4. What do you think these experiments might have to do with flight and airplanes? ______________________

Note To The Teacher: Use with "An Uplifting Experience" on page 9.

Name ____________________

Test Pilot

Exciting news! You've just been hired as the new paper-airplane test pilot. It is your job to determine what makes some paper planes go farther than others. Make a paper airplane using a sheet of typing paper and the directions below. Then throw your paper airplane according to each set of flight instructions listed in the chart below. Record the data from each flight by checking off or filling in the appropriate responses for each test flight.

Directions For Making A Paper Airplane:

Step 1: Fold paper in half as shown in Fig. 1.
Step 2: Fold corner as shown in Fig. 2.
Step 3: Fold same corner again as shown in Fig. 3.
Step 4: Fold same corner once again as shown in Fig. 4.
Step 5: Repeat Steps 2–4 on the unfolded side. (See Fig. 5 for the final airplane.)

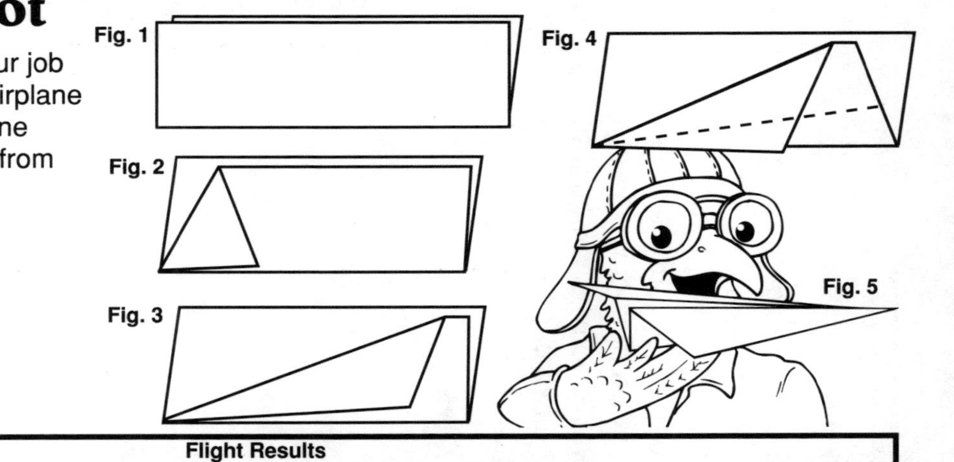

Flight Instructions	Flight Results						
	Directions			Distance	Stability		Other Comments
	Right	Left	Straight		Yes	No	
Flight #1: Fly plane just as it is.							
Flight #2: Open plane slightly along center fold before test flight.							
Flight #3: Attach one small paper clip near the front of the plane on the fold.							
Flight #4: Remove paper clip and attach it to the fold near the back of the plane.							
Flight #5: Attach paper clips to fold at both the front and the back of the plane.							
Flight #6: Remove paper clips. Then cut two slits (about 1/2-inch apart) on back end of each wing on either side of center line. Fold both of the resulting flaps up.							
Flight #7: Fold both flaps down.							
Flight #8: Fold one flap up and one flap down.							
Flight #9: Create a modification of your own to test.							

Note To The Teacher: Provide each student with a copy of this page and one sheet of typing paper. Also have yardsticks or tape measures available for student use.

Name ____________________

Aviation History Month: descriptive writing, art activity

Up, Up, And Away!

Ever since the Montgolfier brothers sent the first hot-air balloon travelers (a sheep, a duck, and a rooster) into the sky in 1783, people have been making balloons that are beautiful sights to behold. Create your own beautiful balloon by coloring and decorating the pattern below. Then cut out your balloon and trace its shape onto a piece of notebook paper. Cut out the pattern you've traced. On the balloon-shaped sheet of notebook paper, write a description of where you would like to go in your balloon, specific things you will see on your way, and who will go with you. Place your decorated balloon on top of your writing. Tape or staple the two pages together at the top so that your story can be read by flipping up the decorated balloon.

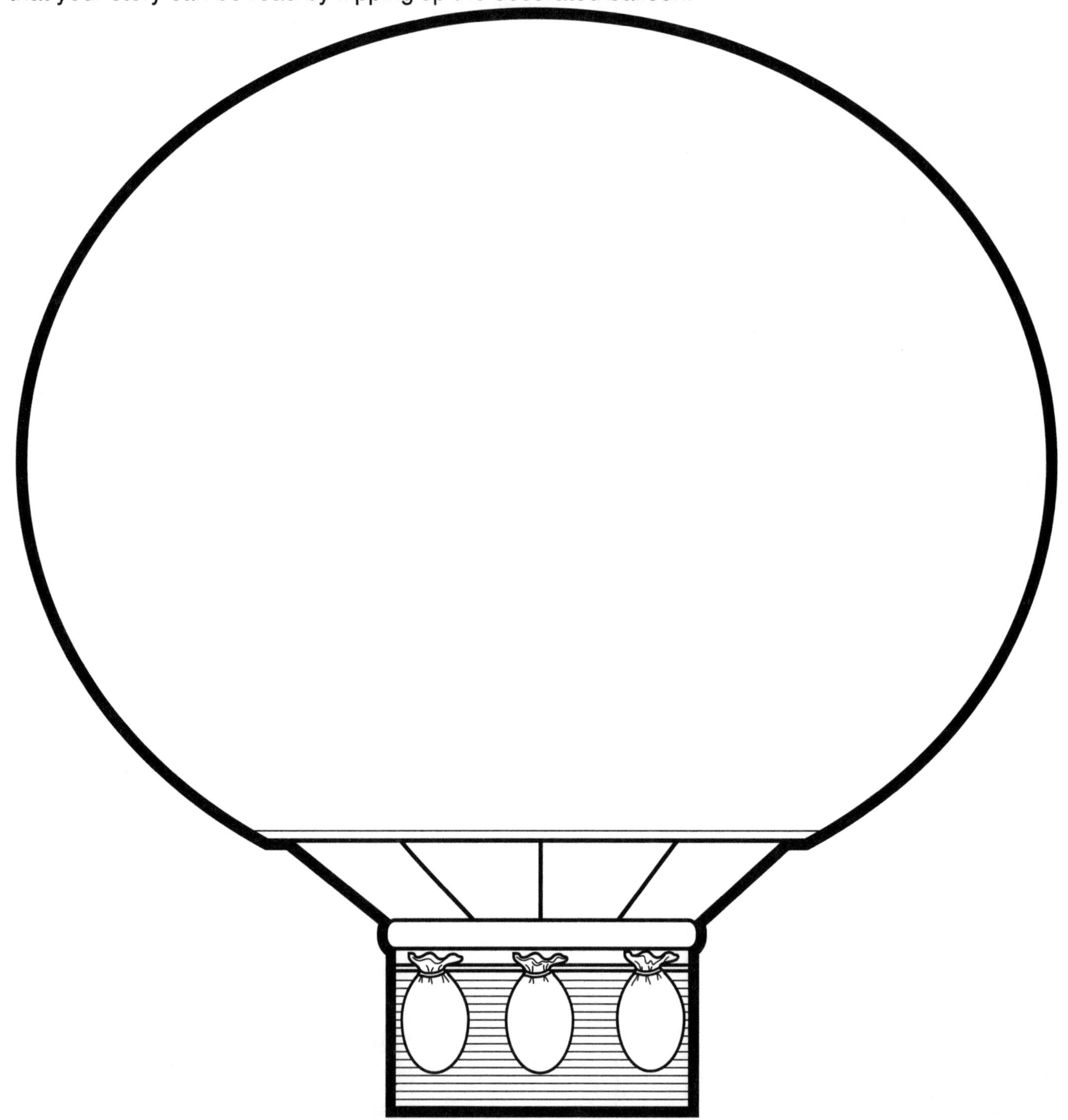

Note To The Teacher: Provide each student with a copy of this page; markers, paints, or crayons; scissors; and tape or a stapler. Post the balloons on a bulletin board for others to see and read.

Name ______________________________

Aviation History Month:
making a model, measurement

Faster Than A Speeding Bullet

No, it's not Superman®. It's *Glamorous Glennis,* the first plane to go faster than the speed of sound. This record was made when the Bell X-1 plane was flown by Air Force pilot Chuck Yeager on October 14, 1947. Create a scale model of the *Glamorous Glennis* by carefully cutting out the patterns below, tracing them onto a sheet of construction paper, and then cutting out the construction-paper patterns. Insert the *wings* into the wide slit in the *body* and insert the *stabilizer* into the small slit in the tail of the body.

The model you've created is to scale. That means that if you measured your model, every two centimeters equals one meter (2 cm = 1 m). Use this scale to help you answer the following questions.

1. The body, or *fuselage,* of your model measures 6.6 cm x 19 cm. What were the dimensions of the real *Glamorous Glennis?* ______________________________
2. The *stabilizer* of your model measures 9 cm x 3 cm. If every two centimeters equals one meter, what were the dimensions of the actual stabilizer of the *Glamorous Glennis?* ______________________________
3. The *wingspan* of your model measures 17 cm. How many meters was the wingspan of the real *Glamorous Glennis?* ______________________________

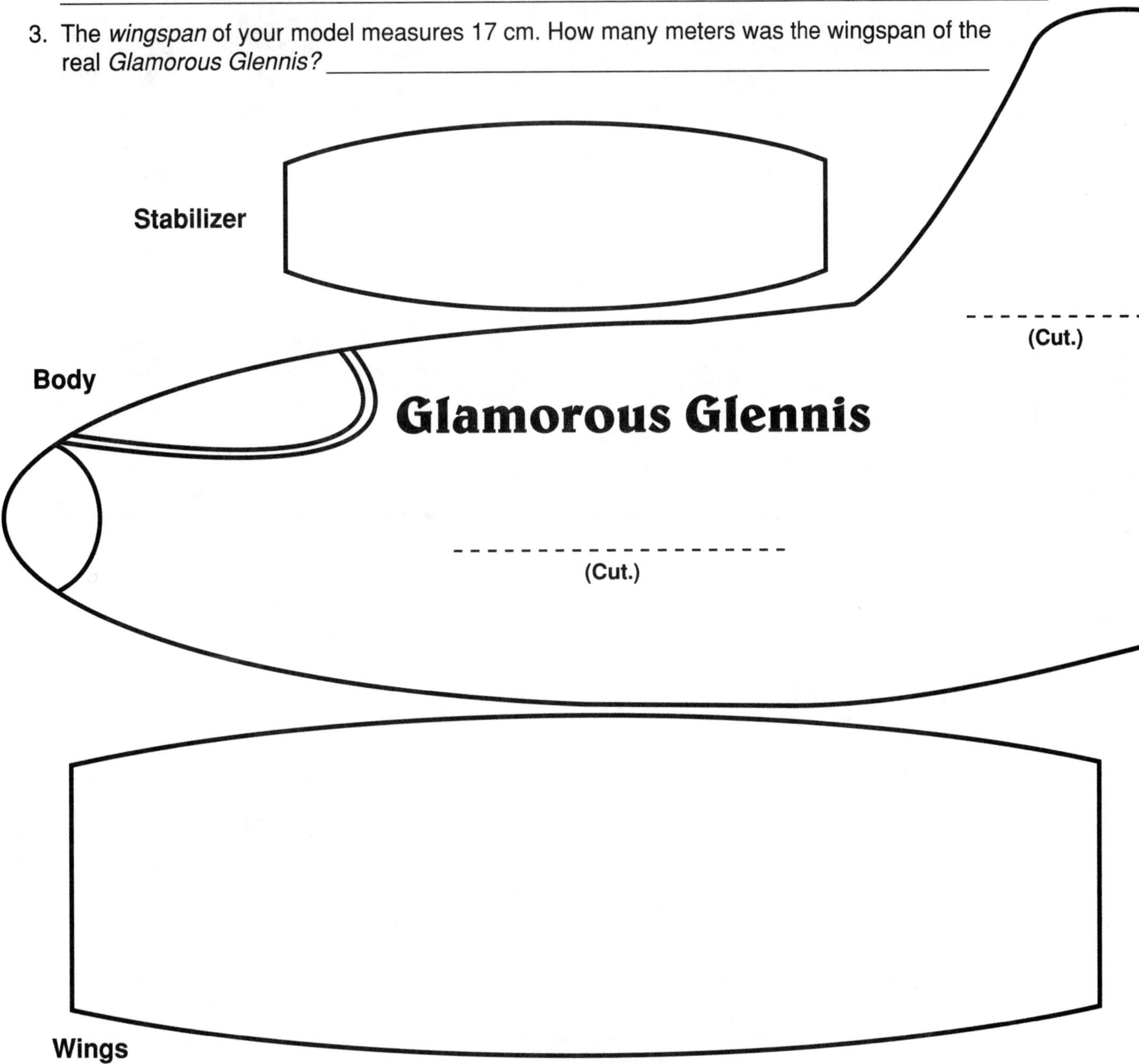

Note To The Teacher: Each student will need one copy of this page, one sheet of construction paper, and scissors.

Name ____

Aviation History Month: character traits

High Fliers

Ever wonder what the pioneers of aviation were really like? To find out, read each description below; then circle the best word that describes the character trait being shown by these pilots and inventors.

1. In 1782, Joseph and Etienne Montgolfier of France noticed that smoke rises, so they tried filling a small silk bag with smoke from a fire and created the first hot-air balloon.
   a. reliable
   b. observant
   c. careful

2. In the early 1800s, Sir George Cayley was the first to realize that a properly shaped wing was the key to making an airplane that would fly. He published his principles of aerodynamics, which would revolutionize flight almost 100 years later.
   a. brilliant
   b. joyful
   c. stubborn

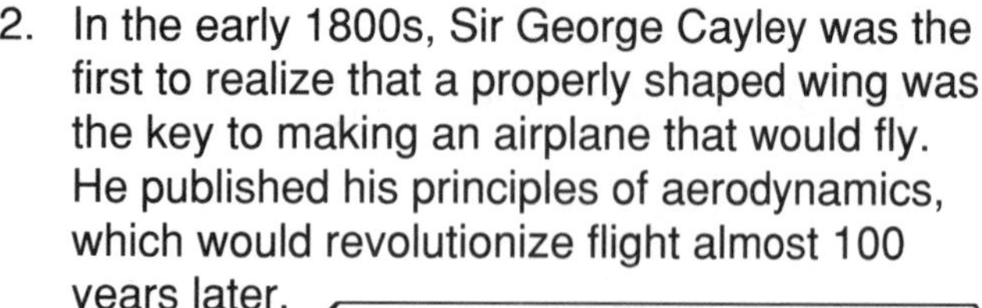

3. Otto Lilienthal made over 2,000 glider flight attempts in an effort to learn more about flight.
   a. dependable
   b. persistent
   c. considerate

4. The Wright brothers pooled their talents and worked together to invent the first manned plane, which flew on December 17, 1903.
   a. kind
   b. careless
   c. cooperative

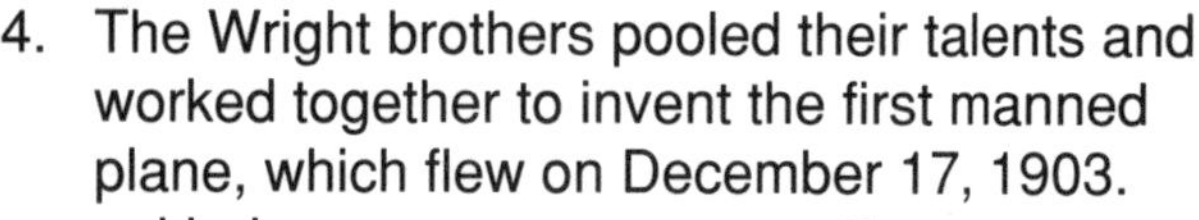

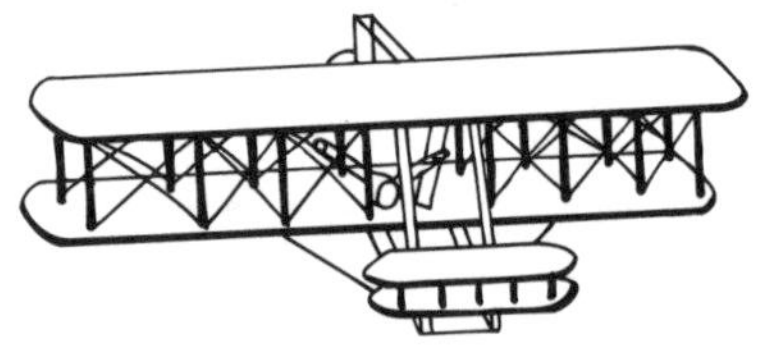

5. Glenn Curtiss thought of putting pontoons on a plane so it could take off and land in the water. He made the first seaplane in 1910.
   a. creative
   b. courteous
   c. sneaky

6. Igor Sikorsky of Russia traveled several times to Paris seeking information on flight and engines. His company built more than 200 planes between 1926 and 1942 and also made 131 helicopters by the end of World War II.
   a. cheerful
   b. proud
   c. hardworking

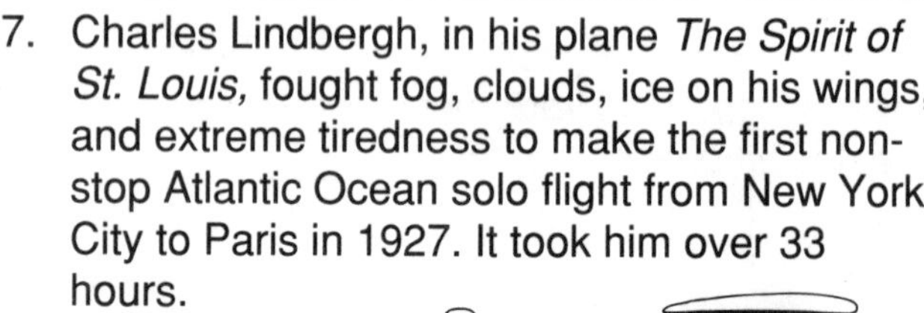

7. Charles Lindbergh, in his plane *The Spirit of St. Louis,* fought fog, clouds, ice on his wings, and extreme tiredness to make the first non-stop Atlantic Ocean solo flight from New York City to Paris in 1927. It took him over 33 hours.
   a. smart
   b. ignorant
   c. determined

8. Amelia Earhart was the first woman to fly many epic flights, such as flying solo across the Atlantic. She wanted to be the first woman to fly around the world in 1937, but her plane disappeared midflight.
   a. considerate
   b. joyful
   c. daring

9. Chuck Yeager was the first to fly faster than the speed of sound, even though other aircraft had broken apart when approaching high speeds in other test flights.
   a. careless
   b. brave
   c. creative

10. The U.S. Air Force and Northrop Grumman unveiled a special type of plane in 1988. This plane could travel secretly past enemy sites at night.
    a. shy
    b. inventive
    c. confident

TOP SECRET

CLASSIFIED

Bonus Box: What is the name of the plane mentioned in number 10 above? Why is this plane so unique?

DANIEL BOONE'S BIRTHDAY

Daniel Boone—American frontiersman, explorer, and militia officer—was born on November 2, 1734, near the present-day city of Reading, Pennsylvania. Because he led waves of settlers westward and because many of his adventures have made their way into the folklore of America, he is celebrated as an American frontier hero.

THE STUFF LEGENDS ARE MADE OF

Introduce your students to the legendary adventures of Daniel Boone with this action-packed activity! Divide students into groups of four or five. Gather several copies of Boone's biographies, at least one for each group. Challenge each group to find a different adventure worthy of turning into a television show about Daniel Boone. After the group chooses a scene, have it write a script that reflects the exciting exploits of this American frontier hero. Allow time for each group to make props and to practice its scene. Have each group perform its episode of "The Daniel Boone Show" for the rest of the class. Or record all the skits on a videotape; then show it to celebrate Daniel Boone's extraordinary life on his birthday!

ON THE LOOKOUT FOR LIVING LEGENDS

By his 50th birthday, long before the days of telephones and television, word of Daniel Boone's exploits had made him a living legend not only in America, but in Europe as well. Widely read literature of the time is a record of his popularity. Lord Byron, the British poet, included a reference to Daniel Boone in his work *Don Juan,* and later, James Fenimore Cooper based heroes in his *Leatherstocking Tales* on Boone.

Put your students on the lookout for living legends in their own time! Have each student choose a living, modern-day inspiration to research. Have each student write a detailed account of the inspirational qualities his living legend possesses in the form of a poem, a song, or an essay. Then have the student create an award designed to suit the accomplishments of the person (for example, a bat for Sammy Sosa). Collect the awards on a bulletin board as shown for a display that's sure to inspire greatness!

IT'S IN THERE SOMEWHERE

The problem with the story of Daniel Boone's life is that there are so many versions of it, each one more incredible than the last. Many authors tell the same story with very different details. Some leave out, add to, or change events, making it difficult for the reader to know what really happened. This kind of confusion makes it necessary for a reader to look deeper for the truth, which can often be hidden by error and legend. One way to do this is to read more than one account of the same story to see what details appear in each. To have students do this, provide each student with a copy of page 17. Direct the student to read both accounts of the story about Daniel Boone, then complete the reproducible activity "Boiling Down A Legend" on page 18. They're sure to find the truth: it's in there somewhere!

Name ______________________

An Incredible Journey

Daniel Boone is credited with following and blazing many wilderness trails in his lifetime. Below is a map of the trails he is thought to have followed or made. Use the map scale to measure the approximate distance of each trail; then write your answers in the space provided.

1. Daniel Boone moved with his family from Exeter, Pennsylvania, to the Shenandoah Valley near Culpepper, Virginia. How far did he travel? ______________
2. From Virginia, the Boone family moved to the Yadkin River valley in North Carolina. This journey was about ______________ miles.
3. If Boone made a trail from the Yadkin River valley through St. Augustine, Florida, and then on to Pensacola, Florida, about how far did he travel? ______________
4. If Daniel Boone blazed a trail from the Yadkin River valley to the Cumberland Gap area in Kentucky, he would have traveled about ______________ miles.
5. If Boone traveled from Boonesborough, Kentucky, to Fort Detroit, how far did he travel? ______________
6. If Boone traveled from Boonesborough to the Femme Osage District in Missouri, how far did he travel? ______________
7. Boone left Missouri when he was eighty-two years old and traveled west to Yellowstone Lake, Wyoming. About how far did he travel? ______________

Boiling Down A Legend

First Account:

In January 1778, Daniel Boone organized a group of 30 men to collect salt for the preservation of meat and the curing of hides. The government of Virginia had given the group heavy salt kettles to use. After serving a one-month shift, the men would be replaced by another team of workers. This would go on until a year's worth of salt was collected.

Collecting salt was not an easy job. The men had to boil 840 gallons of briny water to produce one bushel of salt. Wood had to be chopped and fires kept burning.

Three scouts kept watch for Indians in the nearby forest. For several weeks, there were no signs of Indians. Over 300 bushels of salt were sent back to the settlement on packhorses. The next team of workers was expected to arrive soon. For once, the Kentuckians seemed to be having a streak of good luck.

On a cold day in February, Daniel hunted, scouted, and checked his beaver-trap lines. With a freshly killed buffalo in tow, he was caught in a snowstorm while returning to camp that night. He thought he heard something following him. Perhaps an animal? He turned to find four Indians gaining on him quickly.

He knew he could not fight off four men alone. Thinking he might be able to jump on his horse and escape, he decided to cut the heavy buffalo from his horse. But when Daniel pulled his knife to cut off the carcass, he discovered that buffalo grease had frozen the blade inside the sheath. He left his horse and began running through the snow. The Indians fired warning shots, and Daniel realized there was no escape. He propped his rifle against a tree. While making a sign of surrender, he approached the Indians.

Second Account:

In the early winter of 1778, Daniel led 30 men out to gather salt at the Licking River, a salt-rich river about 40 miles north of the fort at Boonesborough. The men began working. They boiled briny water in huge kettles until only salt remained at the bottom. Daniel looked out for Indians as he rode his horse around the working men. During a blinding snowstorm, he was surprised by a small group of Shawnee Indians.

Daniel knew that he would not be able to reload his rifle quickly enough to shoot all the Indians. The only thing he could do was surrender. The Indians captured him and took him to Chief Blackfish at their Indian camp.

Note To The Teacher: Use with "It's In There Somewhere" on page 15 and "Boiling Down A Legend" on page 18. Provide each student with one copy of this page and one copy of the reproducible on page 18.

Name____

Boiling Down A Legend

Some stories about Daniel Boone are part truth, part legend. One way to determine what is truth is to read two accounts of the same event and look closely at both stories for similarities.

Directions: Read both accounts of Boone's experience making salt in 1778. While reading, you'll discover that, in those days, salt was made by boiling down briny water until only the salt was left in the kettle. As you read, try to "boil down" the legend to get to the truth. Use your reasoning skills to decide which details are *probably* true, which *could be* true, and which *might not be* true. Write the details in the appropriate places on the picture; then answer each question below.

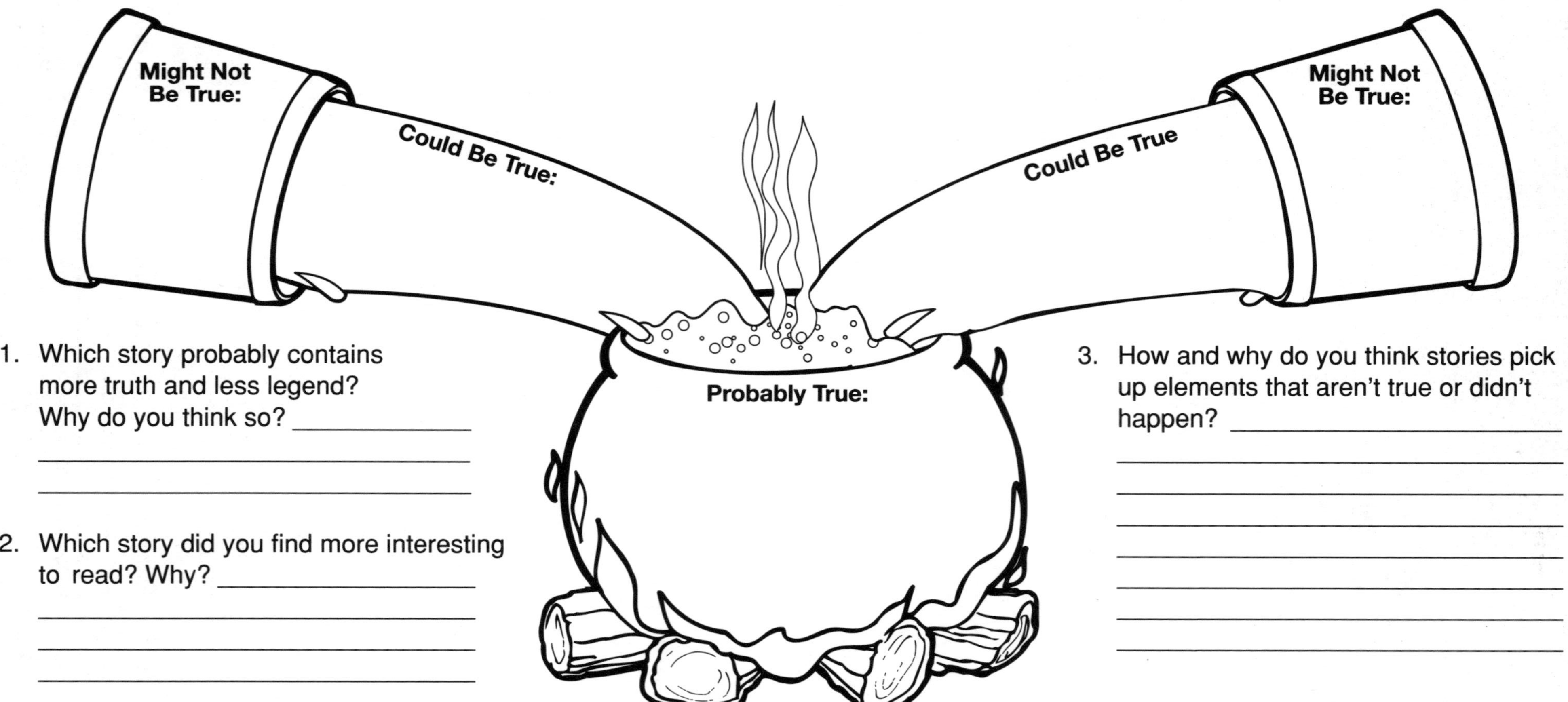

1. Which story probably contains more truth and less legend? Why do you think so? ____________

2. Which story did you find more interesting to read? Why? ____________

3. How and why do you think stories pick up elements that aren't true or didn't happen? ____________

Note To The Teacher: Use with "It's In There Somewhere" on page 15 and "Boiling Down A Legend" on page 17. Provide each student with one copy of this page and one copy of the reproducible on page 17.

Cat Week is celebrated every year during the first full week of November.

"Purr-fect" Pet Care

Celebrate Cat Week by teaching your students a valuable lesson in pet care. Tell the class that an adult female cat can have up to four litters each year, with each litter averaging about six kittens. Have students do a little calculator math to find out how many kittens just ten adult females could produce in a year *(10 x 6 x 4 = 240)*. Then have students come up with ideas to encourage people to be more responsible pet owners. As a follow-up, ask a local veterinarian to talk to your class about caring for cats.

High-Flying Feline

A cat named Felix escaped from her box in the cargo hold of a Boeing 747 while flying from Frankfurt, West Germany, to Los Angeles. She logged 179,000 miles over three continents and made 64 stops before airline personnel discovered her. Direct each student to figure out the average number of miles Felix traveled between stops. Have each student write a story about one of Felix's adventures. Then bind the stories in a class book titled "Felix's Fabulous 'Tails.' "

Another Incredible Journey

Tiger the cat arrived home in Dubuque, Iowa, after a 250-mile journey from Wausau, Wisconsin, where he was lost eight months earlier during his owners' summer vacation. His owners were thrilled to see him again, but they wondered how their pet had crossed the Mississippi River.

Divide your class into groups of three or four students. Have each group develop "Tiger's Tale—The Great Adventure Story," describing just how the cat did find his way home. Ask each group to perform its version of "Tiger's Tale." Then have the students compile all the scenarios into a class book.

Feline Phrases

Have a little feline fun with the following activity on idioms! Each sentence below contains an *idiom*—a phrase whose words taken together often have little or nothing to do with the meaning of the words taken one by one. Each ball of yarn below is labeled with a definition of one of the common idioms listed in the center of the page. Use the context clues found in each sentence to match the idiom with a definition in one of the balls of yarn. Write the letter of the corresponding ball of yarn on the appropriate blank beside each sentence.

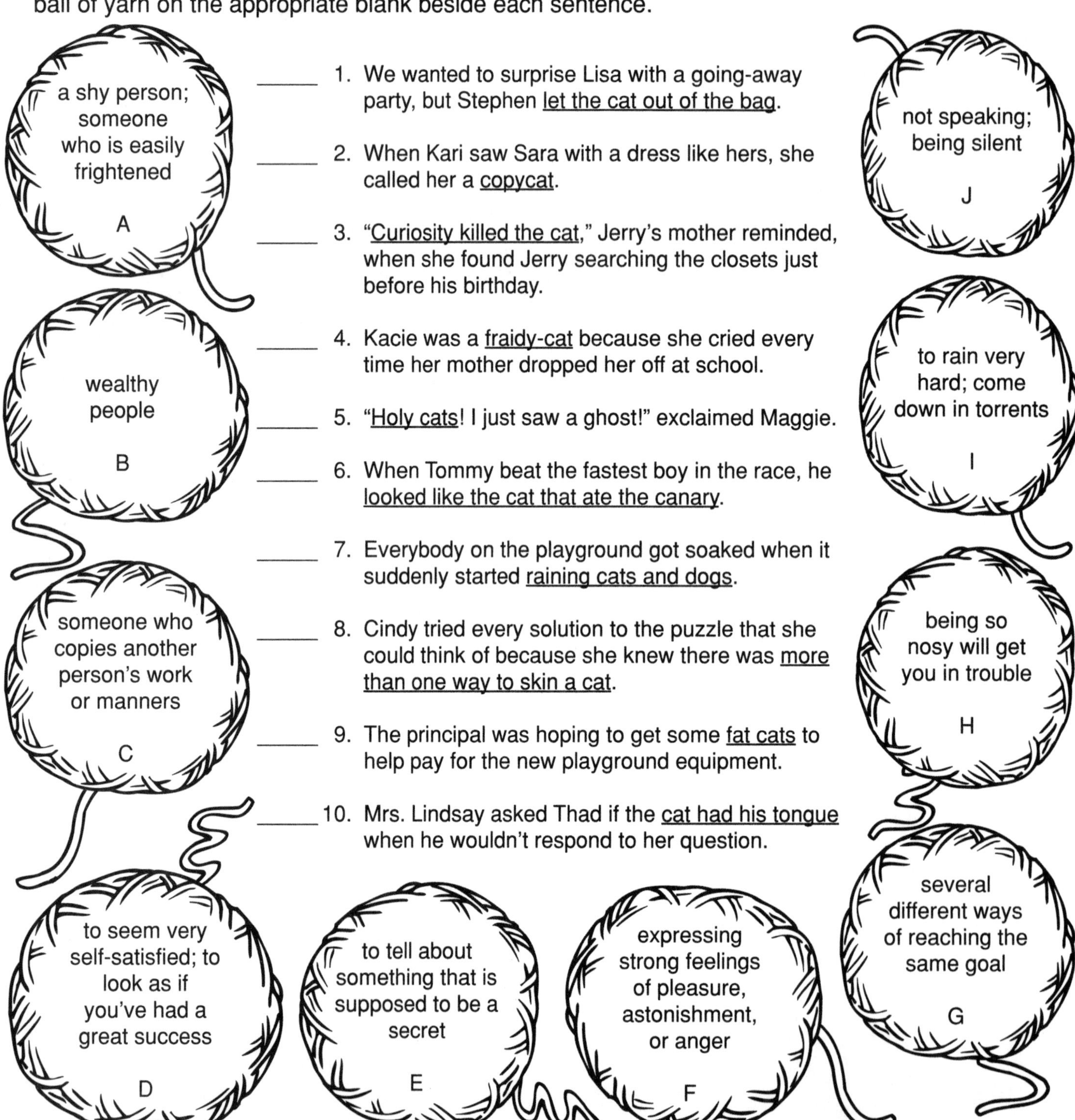

_____ 1. We wanted to surprise Lisa with a going-away party, but Stephen let the cat out of the bag.

_____ 2. When Kari saw Sara with a dress like hers, she called her a copycat.

_____ 3. "Curiosity killed the cat," Jerry's mother reminded, when she found Jerry searching the closets just before his birthday.

_____ 4. Kacie was a fraidy-cat because she cried every time her mother dropped her off at school.

_____ 5. "Holy cats! I just saw a ghost!" exclaimed Maggie.

_____ 6. When Tommy beat the fastest boy in the race, he looked like the cat that ate the canary.

_____ 7. Everybody on the playground got soaked when it suddenly started raining cats and dogs.

_____ 8. Cindy tried every solution to the puzzle that she could think of because she knew there was more than one way to skin a cat.

_____ 9. The principal was hoping to get some fat cats to help pay for the new playground equipment.

_____ 10. Mrs. Lindsay asked Thad if the cat had his tongue when he wouldn't respond to her question.

Bonus Box: What do you think the phrase "while the cat's away, the mice will play" means? Write your answer on the back of this page.

Name ______________________________

A "Purr-fect" Cat

Have you ever wondered what a cat would say if it could talk and tell you a little bit about itself? Imagine that the cat below has human qualities. Fill in each blank with information about the cat. Then dress the cat according to his or her character, adding creative details. For example, if your cat likes sports, you may show him or her holding a baseball bat and wearing a cap.

Name: ______________________________

Nickname: ______________________________

Address: ______________________________

Place of birth: ______________________________

Family members: ______________________________

Job description: ______________________________

Pets: ______________________________

Favorite TV show: ______________________________

Favorite hobby/sport: ______________________________

Favorite snack food: ______________________________

Favorite song: ______________________________

Favorite book: ______________________________

Favorite holiday: ______________________________

Other: ______________________________

____

Bonus Box: On another sheet of paper, write a story about the cat you've described above.

Note To The Teacher: Duplicate one copy of this page for each student. Supply each student with a pencil, markers or colored pencils, scissors, glue, and a sheet of 9" x 12" construction paper. After each student completes the activity, have him cut out his cat and description paper. Then direct the student to glue his cutouts to the sheet of construction paper. Post each student's work on a wall or bulletin board titled "Positively 'Purr-fect' Cats."

Name ______________________________

Big Cats, Little Cats

The family tree of cats is divided into two sections—big cats and little cats. Each cat has different characteristics that make it unique from another. Match each cat illustrated at the bottom of the page with the appropriate character traits by cutting out each illustration below and pasting it onto the appropriate box beside each description.

1. It is a little cat that lives in deserts and mountain areas. It is the size of a housecat and has long, silky fur. This cat can bark like a dog or hoot like an owl.
2. This striped cat is the largest cat in the world. It makes its home on grassy plains, in swamps, and in forests.
3. It belongs to the same family as the bobcat. Its large, furry feet are like snowshoes. These special feet keep the cat from sinking when walking in the snow.
4. This big cat lives alone in a hot, wet forest called a rain forest. It comes in different colors and sizes but usually has spotted fur.
5. This little cat also lives in the rain forest. It will use its teeth and claws to pluck the feathers from a bird before eating it.
6. This pet cat is born without a tail. It has muscular rear legs that are longer than its front legs and runs with a rabbitlike hop.
7. It is a big cat with a loud roar. It is sometimes called the King of the Beasts. It is the only cat that lives in a family.
8. Another name for this cat is a desert lynx. It is a fierce-looking cat that hunts small antelopes, hares, and birds.
9. This longhaired cat is the largest of all pet cats. It has a fluffy, striped tail that resembles a raccoon's tail.
10. It looks like a leopard, but it is larger and heavier. It lives in a hot place, such as a swamp or forest. This cat also swims well and is good at catching fish.
11. Although this cat is in its own family, it's close to the little cats. It does not roar, but instead lets out a loud yowl that sounds like a human scream. This cat also goes by the names of puma and mountain lion.
12. This fast, graceful cat with long legs lives in hot grassland areas. Some are black, but most are orange-yellow with a pattern of spots and stripes.

tiger	lion	leopard	jaguar	ocelot	manul
caracal	lynx	serval	Manx	Maine coon cat	cougar

Bonus Box: Choose one of the cats above. Find five other facts about the animal—such as its physical traits, habitat, food sources, predators, special abilities, or other interesting facts. Illustrate these facts on the back of this sheet.

 Note To The Teacher: Duplicate one copy of this page for each student. Provide each student with scissors, glue, and appropriate reference materials.

SANDWICH DAY

Sandwich Day is celebrated on November 3 to honor the inventor of the sandwich, John Montague, Fourth Earl of Sandwich, who was born on that date in 1718.

My Favorite Hero

Inform your students that not only can a *hero* be a courageous person, but it can also be a sandwich. Have your students brainstorm a list of sandwich ingredients. Record their responses on the board. Then instruct each student to choose a combination of ingredients from the list that she feels will make the ideal sandwich. Also remind each student to decide on what kind of bread or roll she'll use to serve her sandwich. Provide each student with one plastic sandwich bag, one unlined index card, and crayons or markers. Have her write the name and recipe of her perfect sandwich on one side of the card and draw a picture of the sandwich on the other side. Instruct each student to put her completed card inside her sandwich bag. Display the sandwich bags on a bulletin board titled "Happy Sandwich Day!"

Tempting Tidbits

Wrap up Sandwich Day by having each student create a tiny version of his favorite sandwich. Start a sandwich sign-up sheet and instruct students to bring in one ingredient each, such as one can of olives, a jar of mustard, etc. Divide the students into small groups. Then divide the sandwich ingredients equally among each group. For condiments, fill small paper cups with enough ketchup, mustard, or mayonnaise to supply each group. Also supply each group with plastic knives, napkins, and paper plates. Instruct each group to create as many different types of sandwiches as it can. Set a timer for 15 minutes and let the creating begin. After the allotted time has elapsed, have each group describe each sandwich it has created. Then quarter the sandwiches so that each student may sample at least one type of sandwich. Bon appétit!

Fill 'er Up

Bite into Sandwich Day with a memory word game that's sure to challenge your students. Read aloud to your class the following sentence: "The Earl of Sandwich is inventing a new sandwich and in it he's putting…" Then call on a student to repeat the sentence aloud and complete the sentence by naming an edible item that begins with the letter *a.* (Example: "…and in it he's putting *anchovies*!") Challenge a second student to repeat the new sentence before adding a food item that begins with the letter *b.* (Example: "…and in it he's putting *anchovies* and *bologna*!") Continue the process with each student until each letter of the alphabet has been used. If you have more than 26 students, have the 27th student start over with the letter *a.*

Name ____________________

I Make A Great Sandwich

Just like a sandwich, there are many layers that make up you—personality, family history, likes and dislikes, talents. Follow the directions below to create a sandwich about you.

Directions: Cut out each part of the sandwich below. Complete each sandwich part by filling in the needed information on the blanks provided. Color each sandwich part; then stack the parts in order with the top slice of bread on top. Secure the finished sandwich by inserting a brad through the ⊗ found in the upper left-hand corner of the top slice of bread. Make sure the brad pierces each sandwich part.

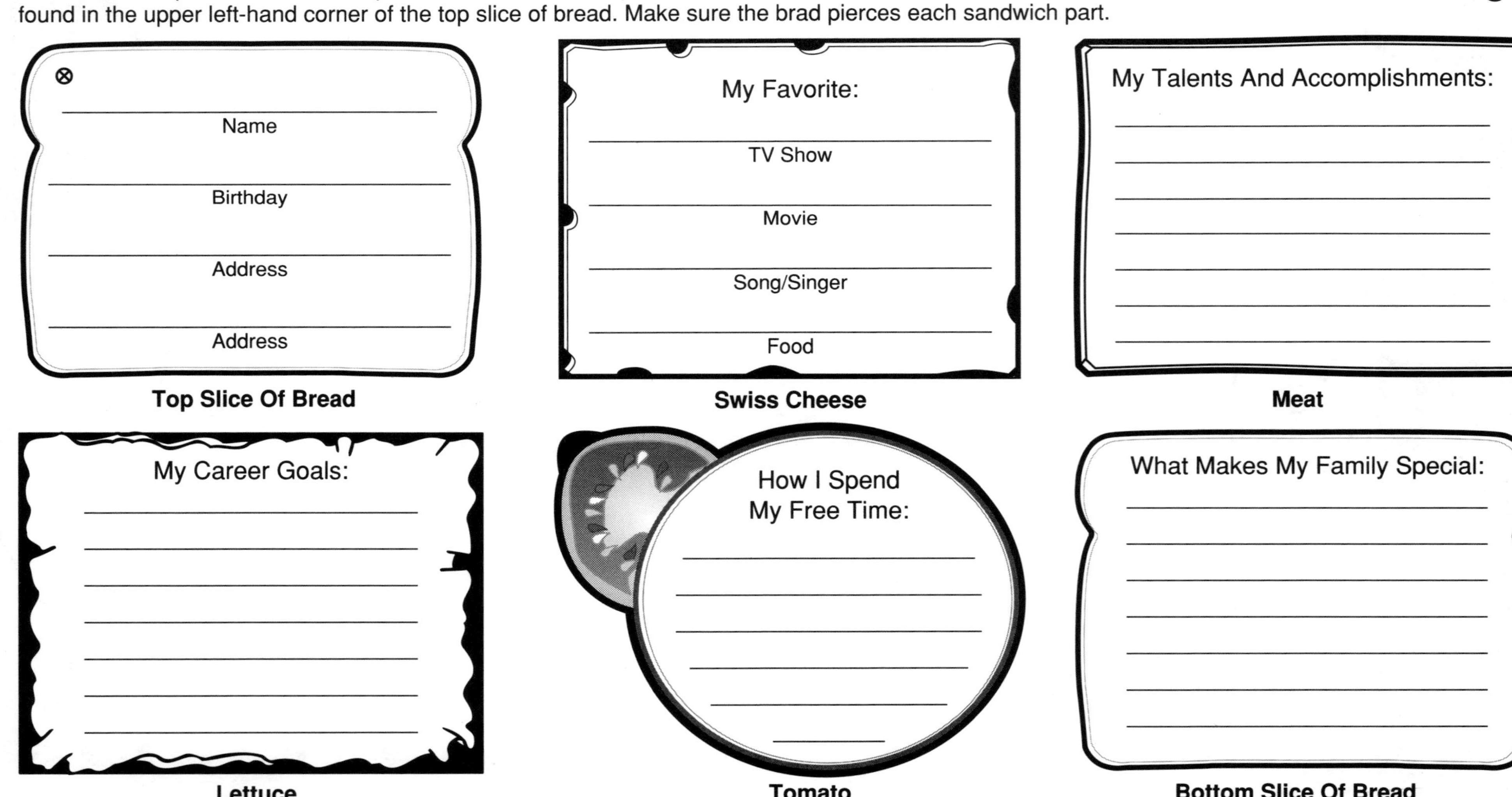

Note To The Teacher: Give each student one copy of this page, scissors, one brad, and crayons or markers.

Mixed-Up Menu!

Mr. Earl has designed a new menu for his sandwich shop. However, he forgot to proofread his work! Help him find all the mistakes before his customers find them first!

Directions: Use the table below to find the proofreading marks you'll need to help Mr. Earl. Use these marks to edit Mr. Earl's menu. When you're done editing, use the back of this page to rewrite the menu correctly.

Common Editing Marks		
symbol	meaning	example
⬭	Check spelling.	The anemal ran.
ℊ	Delete or remove.	She walked the dogg.
⁀‿	Close gap.	I caught a fi sh.
∧	Add a letter or word.	It lives in tree.
/#	Make a space.	The bird fliessouth.
∩∪	Reverse the order.	The animal plants eats.
⊙	Add a period.	She walked home
∧,	Add a comma.	The dog cat, and bird were pets.
∨'	Add an apostrophe.	A deers antlers are huge.
≡	Make capital.	birds eat seeds.
/	Make lowercase.	A Snowshoe hare is white.
( )	Delete some space.	That boy( )is tall.

Eat At Eearls sandwich's Shop!!
todays' Spe shalls

Been And BakonBergger $1.25
Frinch Frie's .... $.95
Milk Shack $1.05
Peanit Buttter Jelley .... $.99
Chips Pota toes .... $.50
16-Ounze Melk .... $.79
Girld CheEse $1.20
Salid Tossed $1.25
Sweat Ice TeaWith Leman .... $.99
Tunerfish On a Role $1.75
Pickel Plat ter .... $.75
Lem inAid .... $.50
Superhero $3.25
Bake d Beenz $1.19
Soda (straw Included) $1.50

20 To Go!

Mr. Sandwich has left you in charge of filling this huge order! He already has the slices of bread ready. Now you have to figure out what to put between the slices!

Example:

Directions: For each problem read the information on the top slice of bread. Then read the information on the bottom slice. Figure out what is missing in the sets. Write the answer in the blank provided.

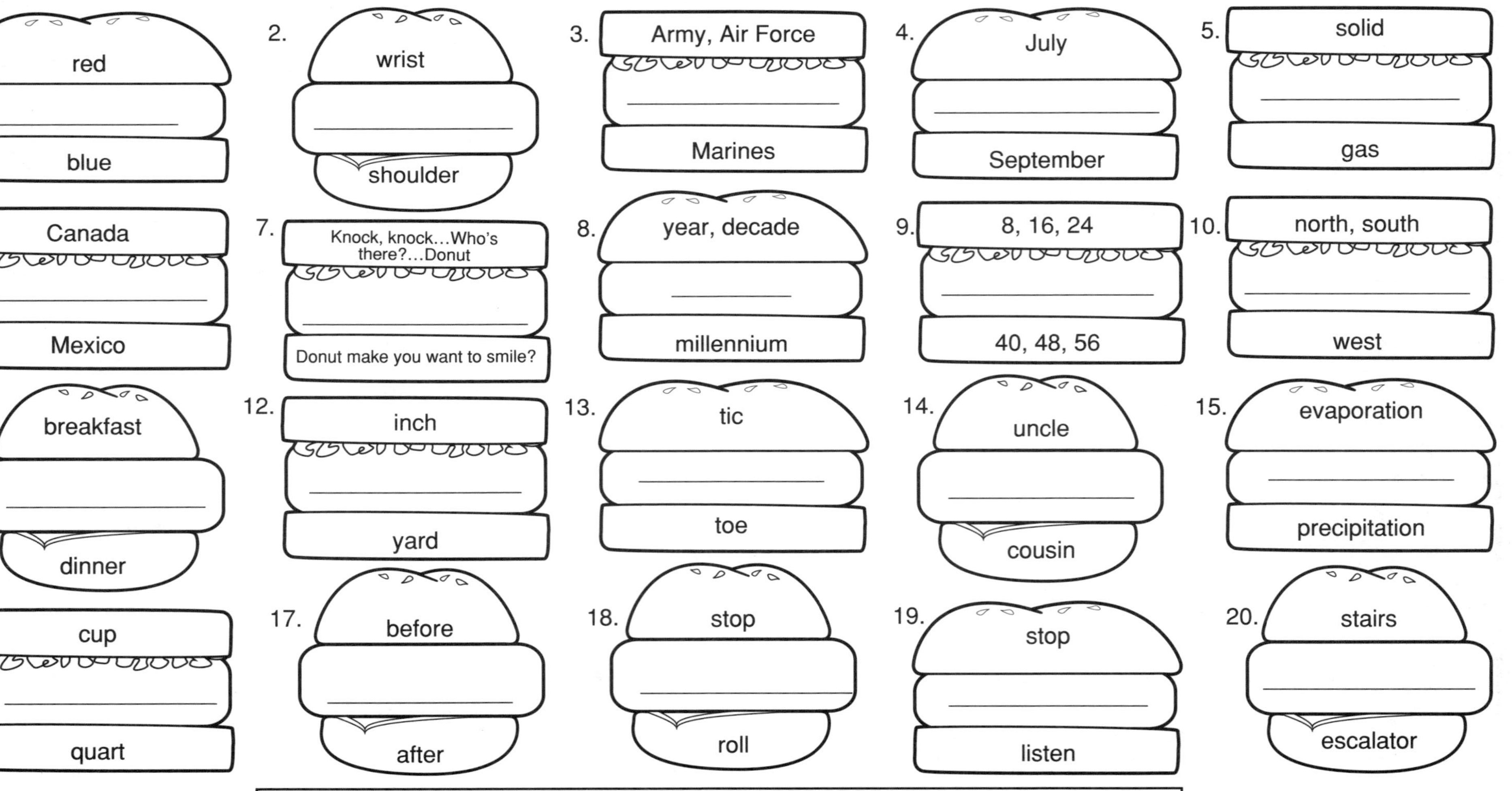

Bonus Box: On the back of this page, create your own set of sandwiches for a friend to solve.

ELECTION DAY

Since 1845, Election Day has been set as the Tuesday after the first Monday in November. On this day, American citizens may vote for their president, vice president, and local officials.

Stepping Into Public Service

Emphasize the politician's role as a public servant and boost your class's community involvement with this critical-thinking activity. Give each group of four students one copy of page 28. Have each group use the questions as a guide to creating a community service project that will become one *plank* in its platform for election. (Explain that real political parties have many planks to appeal to the interests of many voter groups.)

Meet with each group to approve its idea, making any changes before the idea is presented to the class. Once all ideas are approved, have each group create a political advertisement, such as a poster or skit, that presents the problem and how the group plans to solve it.

On presentation day, have each group present its advertisement outlining its project idea. Assign each group a different number; then call for a vote. Have each student cast his vote for the best project idea by writing the group's number on a slip of paper. Collect each student's vote and count the ballots. Then plan a date for the class to begin its new community service project.

Leadership's The Name Of The Game

What are the qualities of a leader? Brainstorm with your students a list of 20 positive qualities of a leader, such as honesty, intelligence, and integrity. Make another list of traits a leader should *not* possess, such as greed or prejudice. Divide students into pairs. Give each pair one copy of page 29, two game markers, and one die. Then instruct each pair to take turns programming its gameboard by writing one positive trait on each *front-runner* square and one negative trait on each *dark horse* square. (You may wish to explain the political jargon at the right.) Sound the starting bell and stand back as your students race to explore which traits can put a leader ahead of the game in politics!

- **front-runner:** someone who is most likely to win an election
- **dark horse:** a candidate who has little chance to win
- **toss one's hat in the ring:** to announce one's candidacy for political office
- **landslide:** an overwhelming victory during a political election

Names____

Election Day: community service project planning

Stepping Into Service

Elected leaders are sometimes called *public servants* because it is their job to help the citizens who elected them. These officials look for problems citizens are having and try to find solutions. You don't have to wait to be **elected** to become a public servant. Just follow these steps to plan a project to help your community right now!

1. Choose a name for your group.
2. Appoint a secretary to take notes. Brainstorm a list of problems for the secretary to record on a sheet of paper. Think of a problem in your school or community that your classmates can solve together. Is there trash on the playground? Is there a vacant lot in town that needs cleaning up?
3. Discuss possible solutions for each problem. Eliminate those that will require resources or skills your group doesn't have. (Remember that writing letters to politicians and other members of the community asking for help can be part of a solution, too.)
4. With the members of your group, carefully consider the problems and solutions still on your list before choosing just one that you'd like to work on as a class. Work together to complete the form below; then present the form to your teacher for his or her approval.
5. After your teacher approves your plan, prepare advertisements and a speech to present to your classmates.

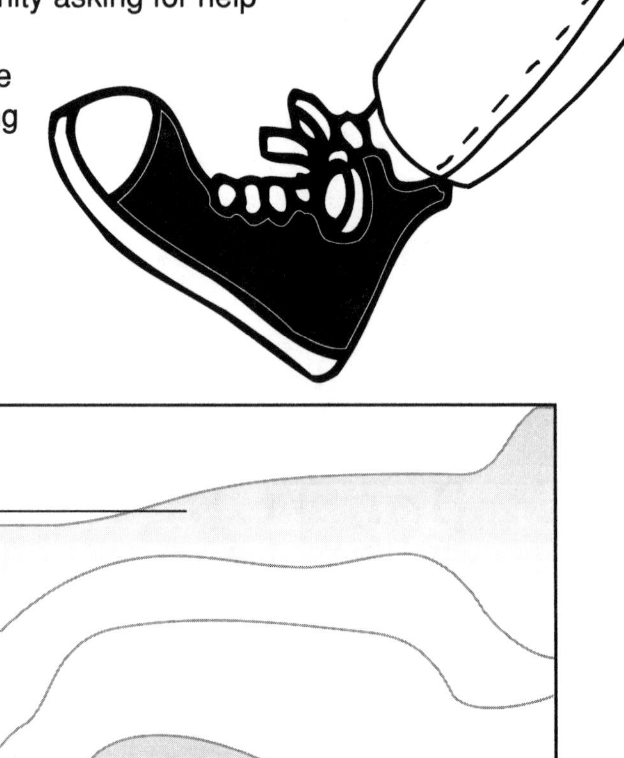

____
(name of group)

The problem we want to solve is

The people affected by this problem are

To solve this problem, we want to

We will need the following people to help us:

We will need the following materials:

Time needed to complete the project:

 Note To The Teacher: Use with "Stepping Into Public Service" on page 27.

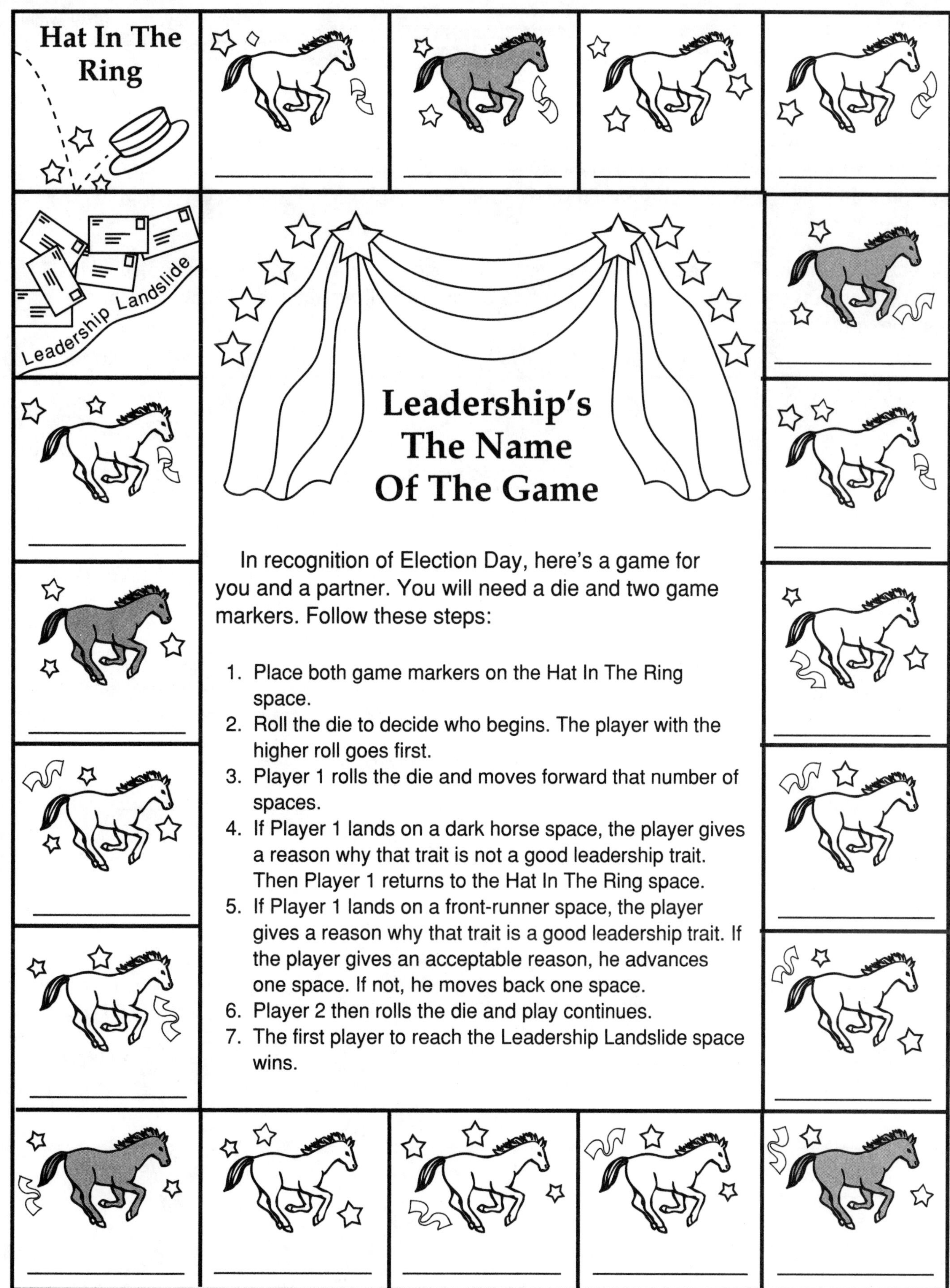

In recognition of Election Day, here's a game for you and a partner. You will need a die and two game markers. Follow these steps:

1. Place both game markers on the Hat In The Ring space.
2. Roll the die to decide who begins. The player with the higher roll goes first.
3. Player 1 rolls the die and moves forward that number of spaces.
4. If Player 1 lands on a dark horse space, the player gives a reason why that trait is not a good leadership trait. Then Player 1 returns to the Hat In The Ring space.
5. If Player 1 lands on a front-runner space, the player gives a reason why that trait is a good leadership trait. If the player gives an acceptable reason, he advances one space. If not, he moves back one space.
6. Player 2 then rolls the die and play continues.
7. The first player to reach the Leadership Landslide space wins.

Note To The Teacher: Use with "Leadership's The Name Of The Game" on page 27.

Name ______________________________

The Right To Vote

Throughout history, many people in the United States have struggled to win the right to vote. For example, Black Americans were not given this right until five years after the Civil War ended. Women were not allowed to vote in most states until 1920, and young adults were not given the right to vote until 1971, when the voting age was lowered to 18. What do you think about kids *your* age having the right to vote?

Directions: On the lines below, write a letter to the editor of a newspaper explaining why kids ages ten and up should have the right to vote. Be sure to include reasons and examples to support your opinion.

Name______________________________

Motto Madness

Presidential candidates often use catchy mottoes or slogans to express their beliefs, goals, ideals, and promises. Candidates often display their mottoes on bumper stickers, buttons, posters, and billboards.

Directions: Read over the mottoes at the right that have been used in past elections. Then create your own original motto by brainstorming topics that are important to you. Write your motto on the bumper sticker pattern below. Enhance your sticker by using bold colors and graphics.

Presidential Mottoes

"Tippecanoe and Tyler, Too."—William Henry Harrison
"It is not best to swap horses while crossing the river."
—Abraham Lincoln
"Let us have peace."—Ulysses S. Grant
"He kept us out of war."—Woodrow Wilson
"Keep Cool with Coolidge."—Calvin Coolidge
"The buck stops here."—Harry S. Truman
"I like Ike."—Dwight D. Eisenhower

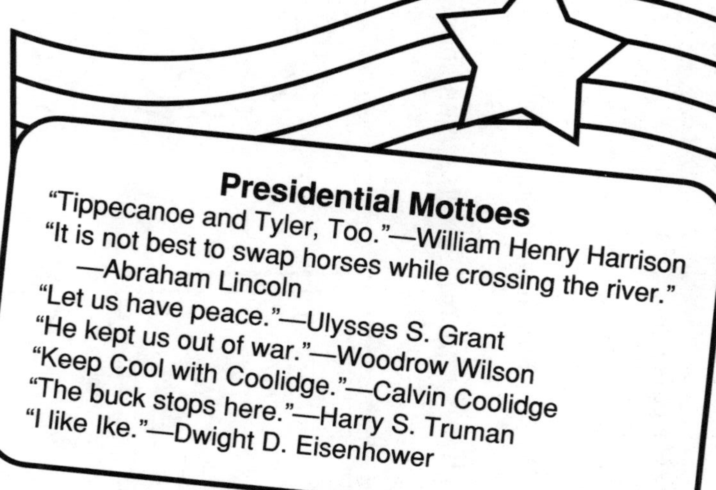

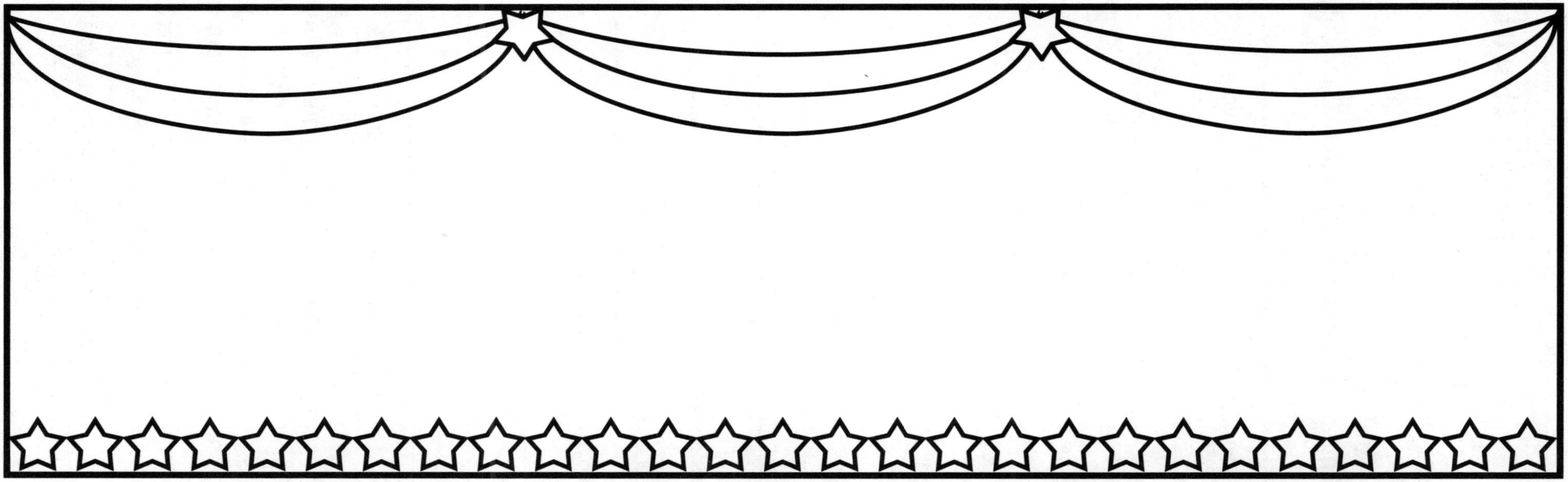

Note To The Teacher: Provide each student with one copy of this page and crayons or markers. Have each student cut out his sticker, mount it to a piece of colorful construction paper, and laminate it. Display the completed stickers on a bulletin board titled "Motto Madness."

Name ______________________________

Every (Electoral) Vote Counts!

To win a presidential election, a candidate must receive at least 270 of the 538 possible electoral votes. In every state but Maine, the candidate that receives the most votes by individual citizens wins all the electoral votes for that state. This winner-take-all system means that candidates have to count carefully if they want to win the election!

Use the map below to help Ms. Bea A. Candidate plan her campaign. Which states should she try hardest to win to become president?

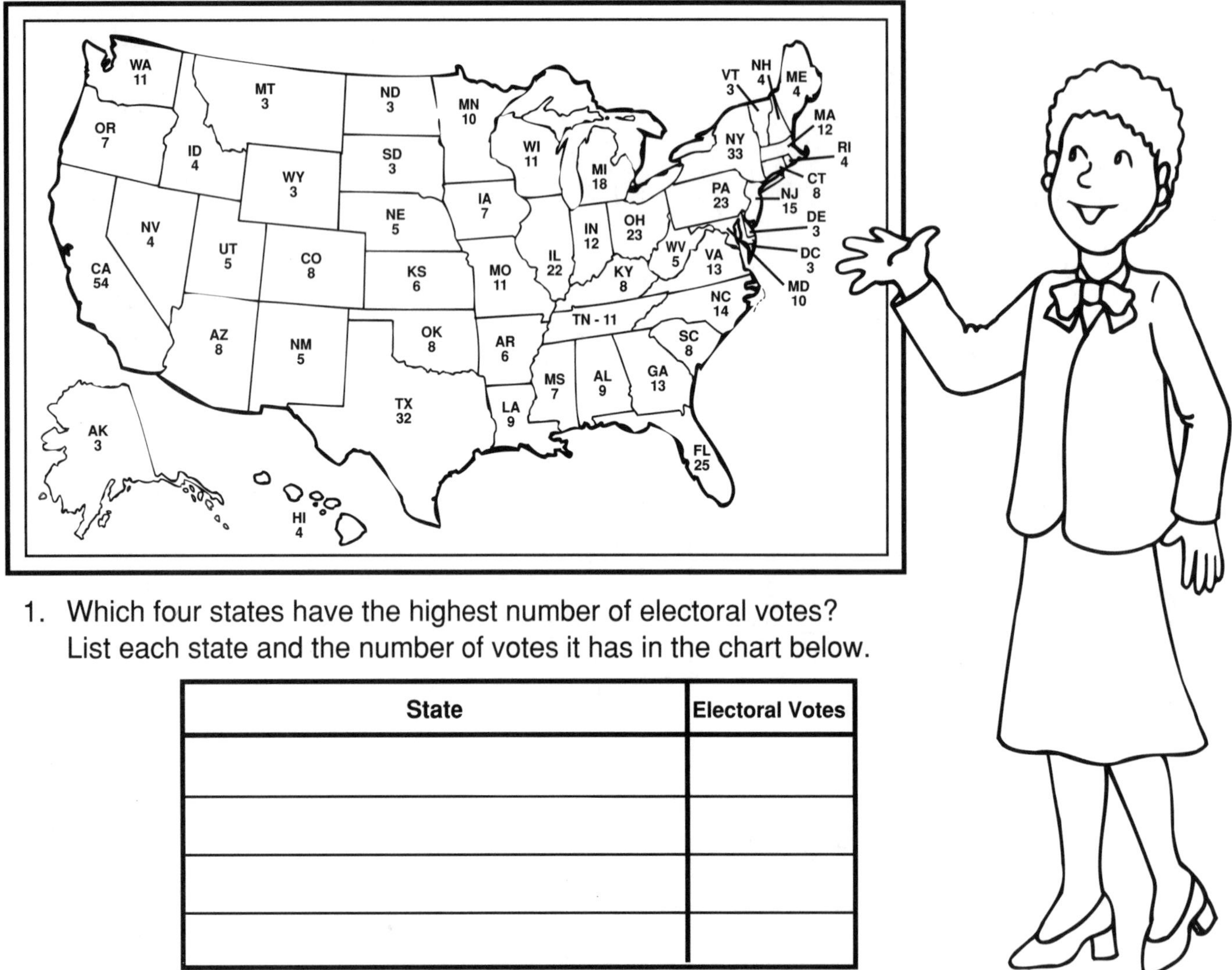

1. Which four states have the highest number of electoral votes? List each state and the number of votes it has in the chart below.

State	Electoral Votes

2. If Ms. Candidate wins all four of these states, how many total electoral votes will she have? ______________

3. To become president, how many more electoral votes will Ms. Candidate need? __________
4. Which states will give her *exactly* this number of electoral votes? Make a list of the states and votes she will need, not including Maine nor the four you listed in number one. Be sure to include her home state of North Dakota in your list! ______________________________

____

____

Bonus Box: Do you think it is possible for a candidate to be elected even if he or she doesn't get the most popular votes? Explain your answer on the back of this sheet.

VETERANS DAY

Veterans Day, observed annually on November 11, was originally called Armistice Day to commemorate the signing of the armistice, or truce, that ended World War I. In 1954, Congress changed the name to include soldiers from other wars. Armistice Day became Veterans Day, a day to honor all the veterans of the U.S. armed forces and to promote world peace.

Heroes All Around

More than 30 percent of the population of the United States is made up of veterans and their families or survivors. Start a search for these heroes by sending students out to survey family members, neighbors, and school personnel using the questionnaire at the top of page 34. After interviewing a veteran, have the student fill out the certificate at the bottom of page 34. Provide a Polaroid® or disposable camera for students to borrow to add photographs to their certificates. To display the certificates, attach dark blue bulletin-board paper along a classroom or hallway wall. Add red curling ribbon, a sprinkling of yellow stars along the edges, and the words "Heroes All Around" across the top. Once all certificates are complete, encourage the class to decide how to organize the display. Suggestions include by rank, by number of years served, by branch of the military, or by wars fought. Allow the students to hang their hero cards for all to see and honor.

Two Minutes To Remember

After the armistice to end World War I had been signed, Australian writer George Honey suggested that people worldwide spend two minutes of silence remembering the soldiers who died in the war. End your study of Veterans Day with a solemn ceremony that incorporates the tradition begun by Honey. Invite a guest speaker—such as a local veteran, a war hero, or someone currently serving in the military—to speak to students. At 11:00, in honor of the cease-fire of World War I that took place at 11:00 A.M. on November 11, 1918, and to honor those who have served in the armed forces, have your students observe two minutes of silence.

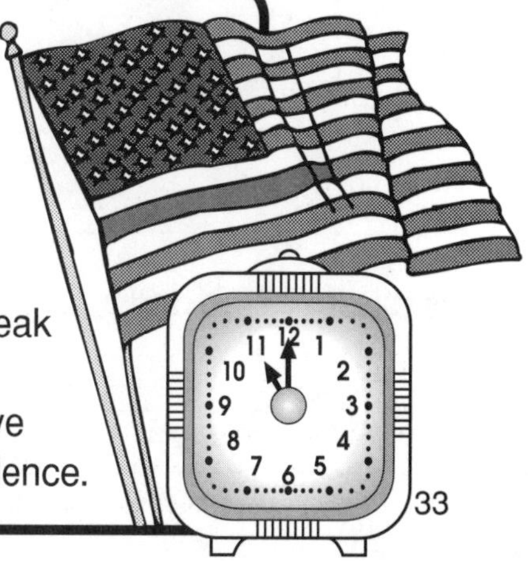

Name ____________________

Veterans Day: interviewing a veteran

Heroes All Around

Use the following questions to interview a local veteran.

1. Name of veteran: ____________________
2. In which branch of the military did you serve? ____________________
3. How many years did you serve? ____________________
4. What rank did you earn? ____________________
5. In which war(s) or conflict(s) did you fight? ____________________
6. What interesting places did you visit while in the military? ____________________
7. What was your job in the military? ____________________
8. What is your job now? ____________________

Name ____________________

Veterans Day: honoring a veteran

(photo or drawing of veteran)

(name of veteran)

is

____________________'s hero!
(name of student)

____
(name of veteran)

served in the ____________ for ________ years. During this time,
(branch) (number)

____
(name of veteran, including rank)

____
(description of job held, war or conflict fought in)

____________________. ____________________
(name of veteran)

is a hero to me because ____________________

____________________.

 Note To The Teacher: Duplicate this page for each student. Use with "Heroes All Around" on page 33.

Name ____

We Remember

The *poppy* is a small red flower that grows wild in the fields of Europe, where many of those who died in the first world war are buried. Follow the directions below to create a card featuring poppies, a symbol of Veterans Day. Give your completed card to a veteran, honoring and thanking him or her for the freedoms you enjoy.

Materials needed:

one 9" x 12" sheet of blue construction paper
two 8 1/2" x 11" sheets of white paper
one 5" x 5" piece of green construction paper
glue
markers
scissors
ruler

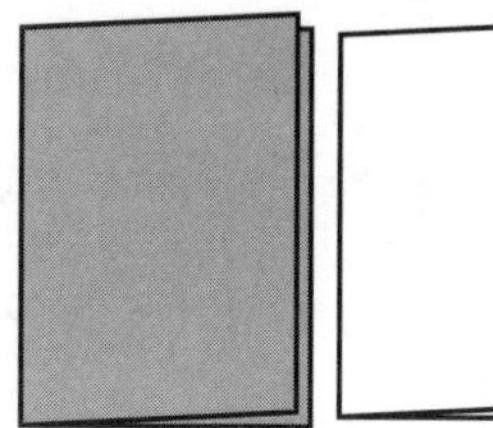

Figure 1

Directions:

1. Fold the blue paper and one sheet of the white paper in half (see Figure 1). Put the blue sheet and the unfolded white sheet aside.
2. Place the folded white paper in front of you so that the folded edge is on your left as shown. Using your ruler, measure 3 1/2" from the bottom of the paper on the folded edge and make a dot. Make a second dot 5 1/2" from the bottom and a third dot 7 1/2" from the bottom of the paper (see Figure 2).

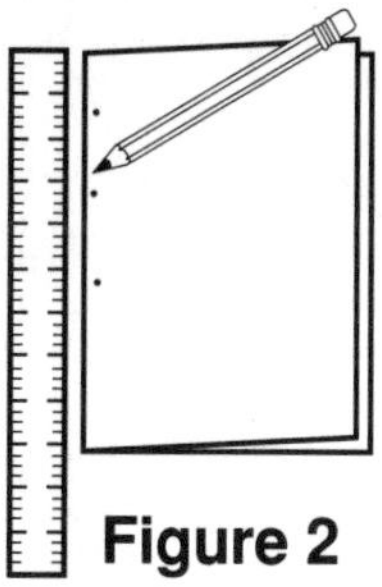

Figure 2

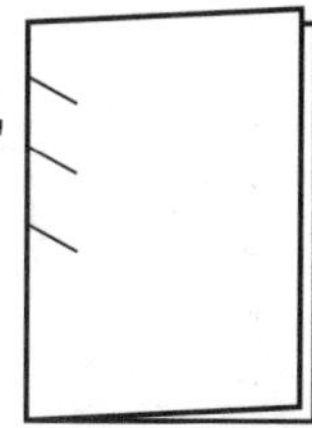

Figure 3

3. Draw a diagonal line about 1" long down from each dot. The lines should be parallel to each other (see Figure 3).
4. Starting from the folded edge, cut the three parallel diagonal lines.
5. Fold the cut strips forward and back again (see Figure 4).

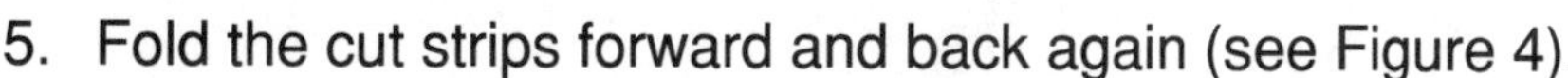

6. Open the folded white sheet of paper. To make the sections pop out, pull each diamond shape toward you and press along the folded lines (see Figure 5). The cut sections will stand out toward you.

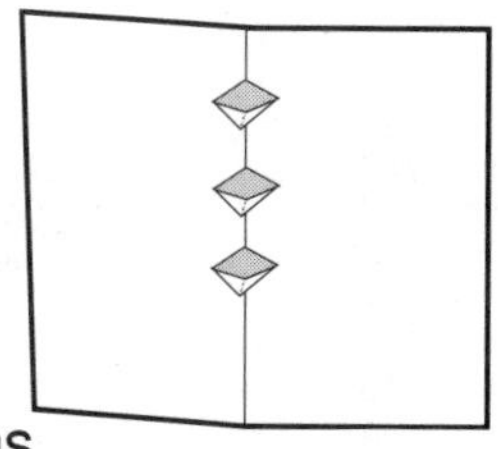

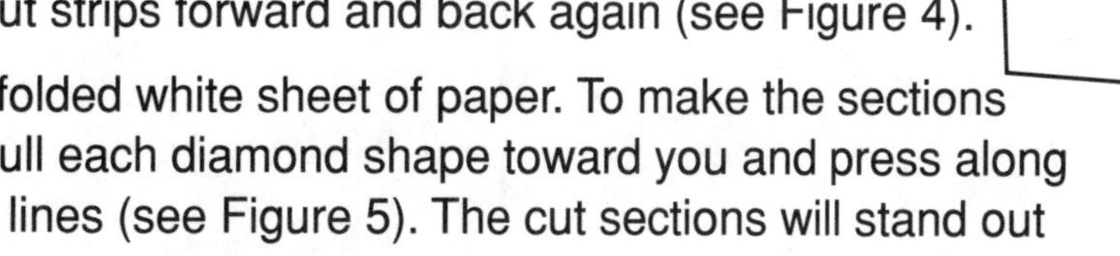

Figure 5

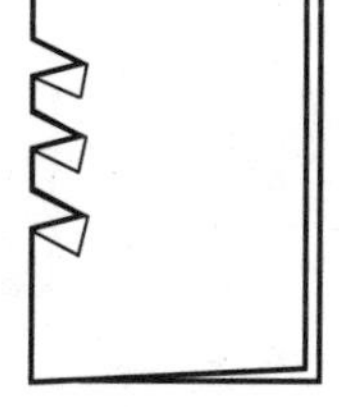

Figure 4

7. Cut three 1" x 1/4" strips from the green paper to make the stems. Apply glue to the bottom of each strip. Place the strips on the pop-up sections as shown and press firmly.
8. On the unused sheet of white paper, draw one small poppy flower for each stem. Color each poppy red, cut it out, and glue one flower to each stem (see Figure 6). Add leaves if desired.
9. Apply glue to the back of the folded white paper but not in the area of the pop-up strips. Insert the white paper in the center of the folded blue paper, which now becomes the outside of your card (see Figure 7).
10. Decorate the outside of the card for a veteran and write a note on the inside, thanking the veteran for his or her service.

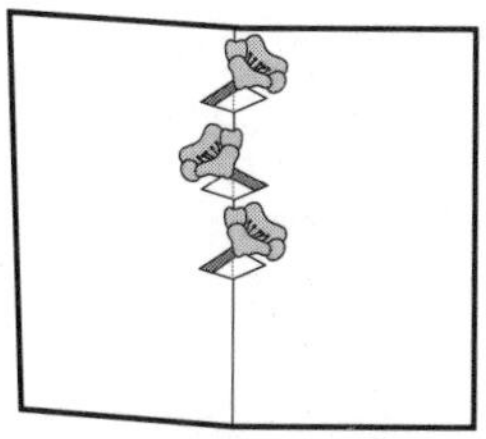

Figure 6

Figure 7

Note To The Teacher: Provide each student with one copy of this page and the materials listed above.

Operation Timeline

Directions: Each of the word problems below can be solved by using either addition or subtraction. Solve each problem and write the operation used and the answer in the blanks provided. After solving each problem, cut the boxes apart. Create a timeline of the history of Veterans Day by gluing the boxes onto another sheet of paper in the order that the events occurred. Color and cut out the soldiers to decorate your timeline.

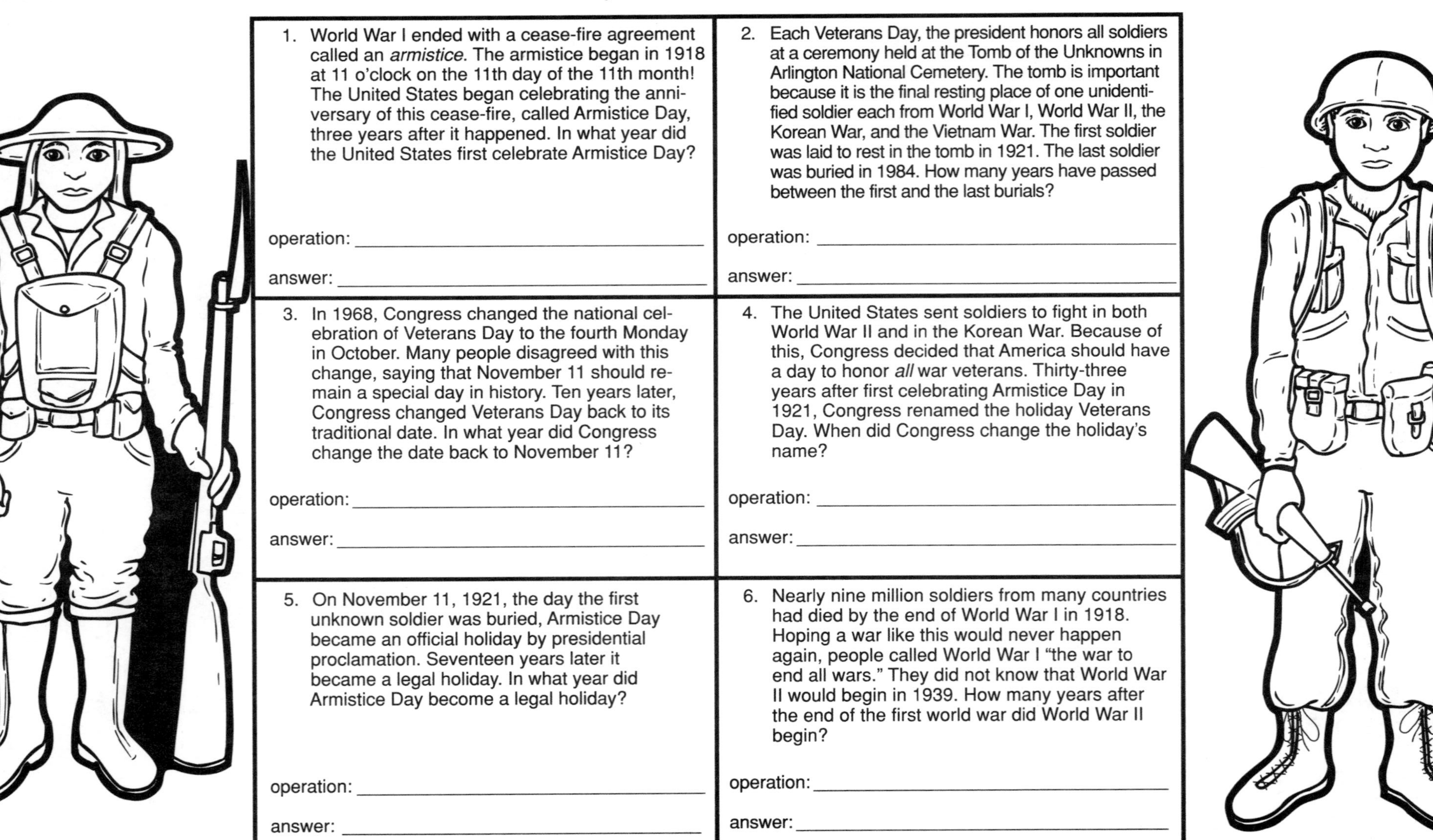

1. World War I ended with a cease-fire agreement called an *armistice*. The armistice began in 1918 at 11 o'clock on the 11th day of the 11th month! The United States began celebrating the anniversary of this cease-fire, called Armistice Day, three years after it happened. In what year did the United States first celebrate Armistice Day?

   operation: ____________________

   answer: ____________________

2. Each Veterans Day, the president honors all soldiers at a ceremony held at the Tomb of the Unknowns in Arlington National Cemetery. The tomb is important because it is the final resting place of one unidentified soldier each from World War I, World War II, the Korean War, and the Vietnam War. The first soldier was laid to rest in the tomb in 1921. The last soldier was buried in 1984. How many years have passed between the first and the last burials?

   operation: ____________________

   answer: ____________________

3. In 1968, Congress changed the national celebration of Veterans Day to the fourth Monday in October. Many people disagreed with this change, saying that November 11 should remain a special day in history. Ten years later, Congress changed Veterans Day back to its traditional date. In what year did Congress change the date back to November 11?

   operation: ____________________

   answer: ____________________

4. The United States sent soldiers to fight in both World War II and in the Korean War. Because of this, Congress decided that America should have a day to honor *all* war veterans. Thirty-three years after first celebrating Armistice Day in 1921, Congress renamed the holiday Veterans Day. When did Congress change the holiday's name?

   operation: ____________________

   answer: ____________________

5. On November 11, 1921, the day the first unknown soldier was buried, Armistice Day became an official holiday by presidential proclamation. Seventeen years later it became a legal holiday. In what year did Armistice Day become a legal holiday?

   operation: ____________________

   answer: ____________________

6. Nearly nine million soldiers from many countries had died by the end of World War I in 1918. Hoping a war like this would never happen again, people called World War I "the war to end all wars." They did not know that World War II would begin in 1939. How many years after the end of the first world war did World War II begin?

   operation: ____________________

   answer: ____________________

NATIONAL GEOGRAPHY AWARENESS WEEK

National Geography Awareness Week is observed each year during the third full week in November.

Remember Your Geography

Teach your students the *mnemonic devices* below to help them remember geographic facts. Then have each student create a mnemonic device of his own to help him remember the states in each physical region of the United States. Record some of the best devices on the board for students to use for easy reference.

- Display the word *HOMES* (Huron, Ontario, Michigan, Erie, Superior) to help remember the names of the five Great Lakes.
- Learn the Great Lakes in order from west to east with the sentence "Super Man Helps Every One."
- The middle states (Minnesota, Iowa, Missouri, Arkansas, Louisiana) can be remembered as MIMAL.
- Encourage students to create a device to remember the names of the four oceans. (Example: Princess Anna Is Awesome.)

Princess Anna Is Awesome.

Latitude And Longitude Fun

Use the playground for this hands-on (and feet) game! Have your students pretend the blacktop is a giant map. With masking tape, mark where the *North Pole, South Pole, prime meridian,* and *equator* would be located. With everyone standing on the equator, call out a marked or unmarked location, such as the name of a country. Instruct the students to move to that location by the count of five. Students who are not at or near the specified location by the count of five are out. Continue playing the game for a specified time or until there is only one person left on the map.

Ingredients:

6 cups creamy peanut butter
3 cups honey
6 cups instant dry milk
4 cups instant oats
green and blue food coloring

Directions: Mix the first four ingredients together in a large bowl. Then divide the mixture in half. Place each half into a separate bowl. Place a few drops of green food coloring into one bowl and mix together. Then place a few drops of blue food coloring into the other bowl and mix together. Refrigerate overnight. This should be plenty of dough for approximately 30 students.

Make Your Land And Eat It Too!

Here's a recipe guaranteed to make geography fun! Use the recipe at the left to make edible clay. After you've prepared the dough, have students thoroughly wash their hands. Give each student a piece of waxed paper; then distribute equal portions of green and blue dough to each student. List several types of landforms on the board. Inform students that the green dough represents land and the blue dough represents water. Then instruct each student to use his colored dough to create each landform. Circulate to see that students are correctly forming each landform. Finally, instruct the students to chow down and enjoy eating their tasty creations.

Name ______________________________

Making Tracks

Make tracks across the United States and learn about some cool landforms too! Use the directions and landform clues. Begin at the symbol on New Mexico. Follow each set of directions and put the correct symbol in the appropriate state on the map. Read each landform clue carefully. Use the clue and other resources to identify the landform and write the name of the landform in the blank provided.

1. **Directions:** Move 1 state west, 1 north, and 1 east.
   Name of state: ____________________
   Landform clue: This snow-capped peak is 14,110 feet above sea level.
   Name of landform: ____________________
   Symbol: ▲

2. **Directions:** Move 1 state east, 1 south, and 1 east.
   Name of state: ____________________
   Landform clue: This site yields about one million gallons of hot water a day.
   Name of landform: ____________________
   Symbol: ●

3. **Directions:** Move 1 state south, 3 states east, and 1 state south.
   Name of state: ____________________
   Landform clue: This is a huge swamp covering over one million acres.
   Name of landform: ____________________
   Symbol: ■

4. **Directions:** Move 1 state north, 1 west, and 2 north.
   Name of state: ____________________
   Landform clue: This is part of the world's longest known cave system.
   Name of landform: ____________________
   Symbol: ✖

5. **Directions:** Move 1 state north to Indiana, 1 west, 1 north, 1 west, 1 south, 1 west, and 1 north.
   Name of state: ____________________
   Landform clue: This landform pays tribute to four famous U.S. presidents and is sometimes called the Shrine of Democracy.
   Name of landform: ____________________
   Symbol: ◉

6. **Directions:** Move 1 state north, 3 west, and 1 south.
   Name of state: ____________________
   Landform clue: This is the deepest lake in the United States.
   Name of landform: ____________________
   Symbol: ★

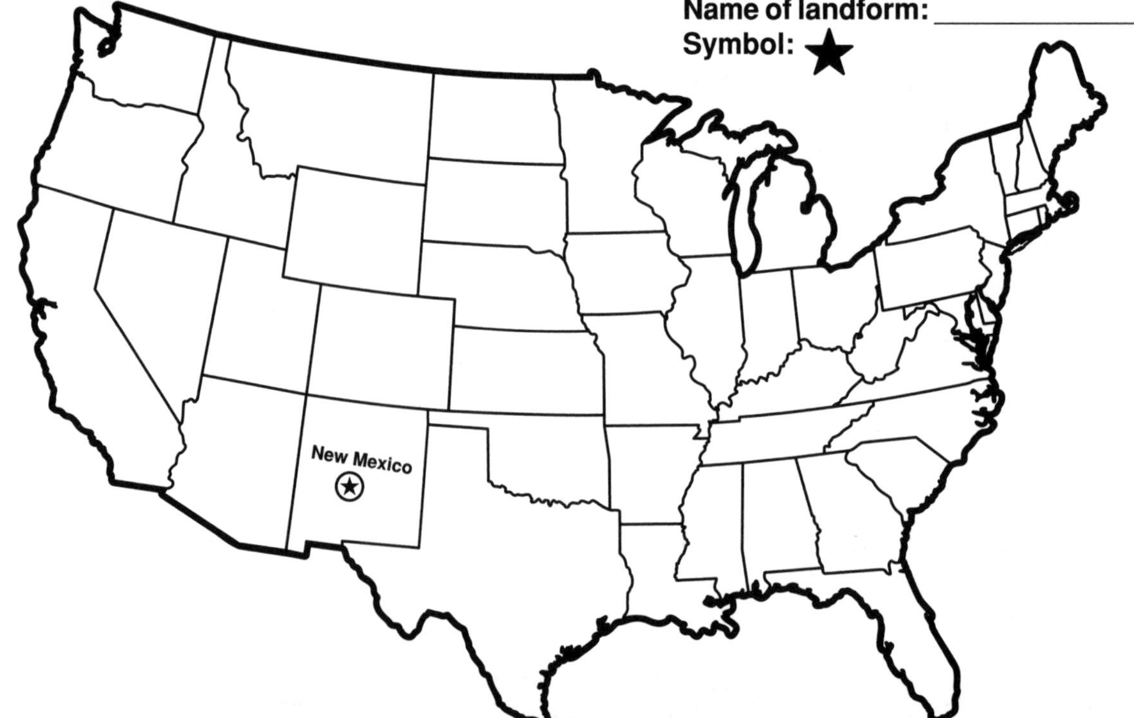

A Booklet Of Land Features

Follow these steps to create a booklet of land features:

Step 1: Fold the paper in half widthwise; then fold it again in the same direction.

Step 2: Fold the paper again but in the opposite direction.

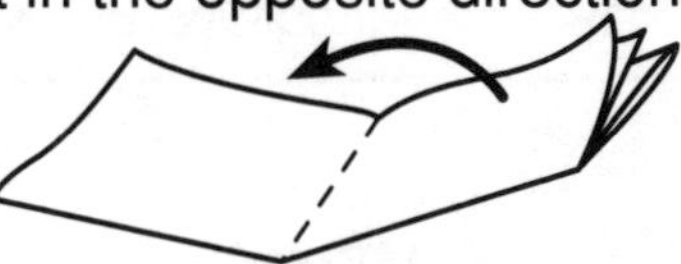

Step 3: Open the paper as shown and make a cut in the center at the fold. Only cut to where the fold lines cross.

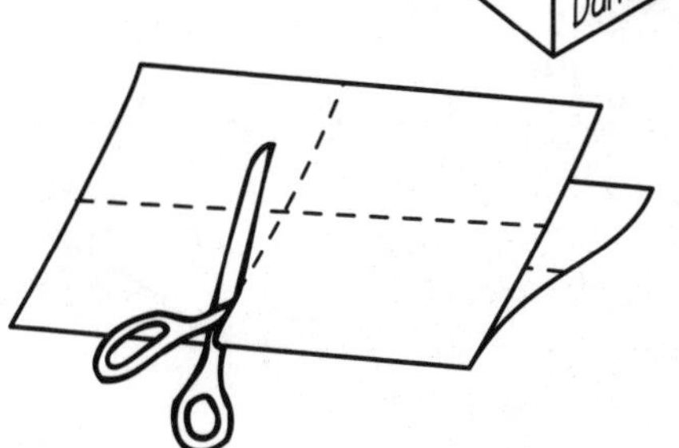

Step 4: Open the paper to a full sheet.

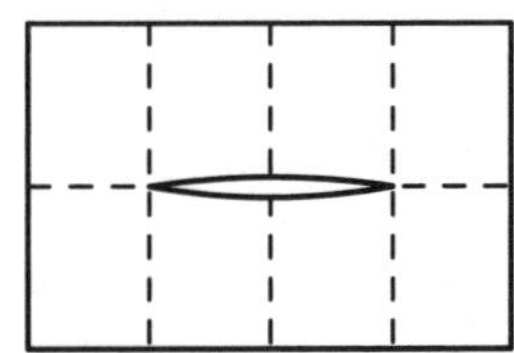

Step 5: Fold the paper as shown. Grab the two outer edges and push in as shown to create a diamond shape in the center. Keep pushing until the two sides meet.

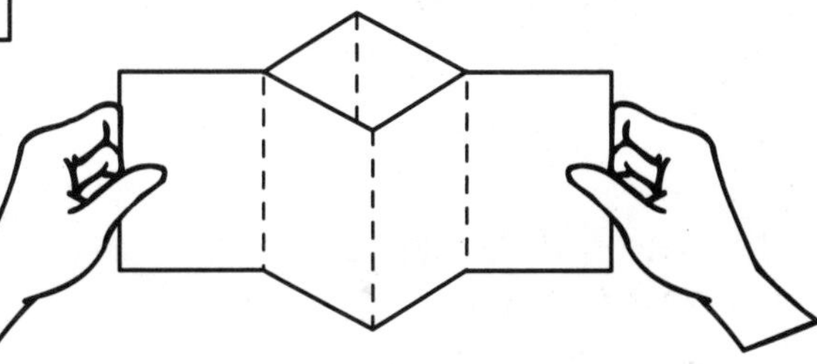

Step 6: Fold all the pages in the same direction to create a booklet.

Step 7: Write the title "Landforms" and your name on the cover of your booklet.

Step 8: Choose seven landforms from the box below. Write each word at the top of a different page in your booklet. Underneath each word write a brief definition and draw an illustration of the landform.

Landforms

- Archipelago
- Bay
- Canyon
- Delta
- Estuary
- Gulf
- Isthmus
- Lagoon
- Mouth, River
- Oasis
- Plateau
- Range, Mountain
- Source, River
- Strait
- Tributary
- Valley

Note To The Teacher: Give each student one copy of this page, one 9" x 12" sheet of white paper, scissors, crayons or markers, and reference materials on landforms.

Name ______________________________

Hemisphere "Ad-VENN-tures"

The Venn diagram is made up of two or more overlapping circles. It can be used in social studies to show the relationship between the world's four hemispheres.

Directions: Look at a map or globe to locate each of the continents and oceans listed below. Write each one in the appropriate hemispheres in the Venn diagram.

- Africa
- Antarctica
- Asia
- Australia
- Europe
- North America
- South America
- Atlantic Ocean
- Pacific Ocean
- Indian Ocean
- Arctic Ocean

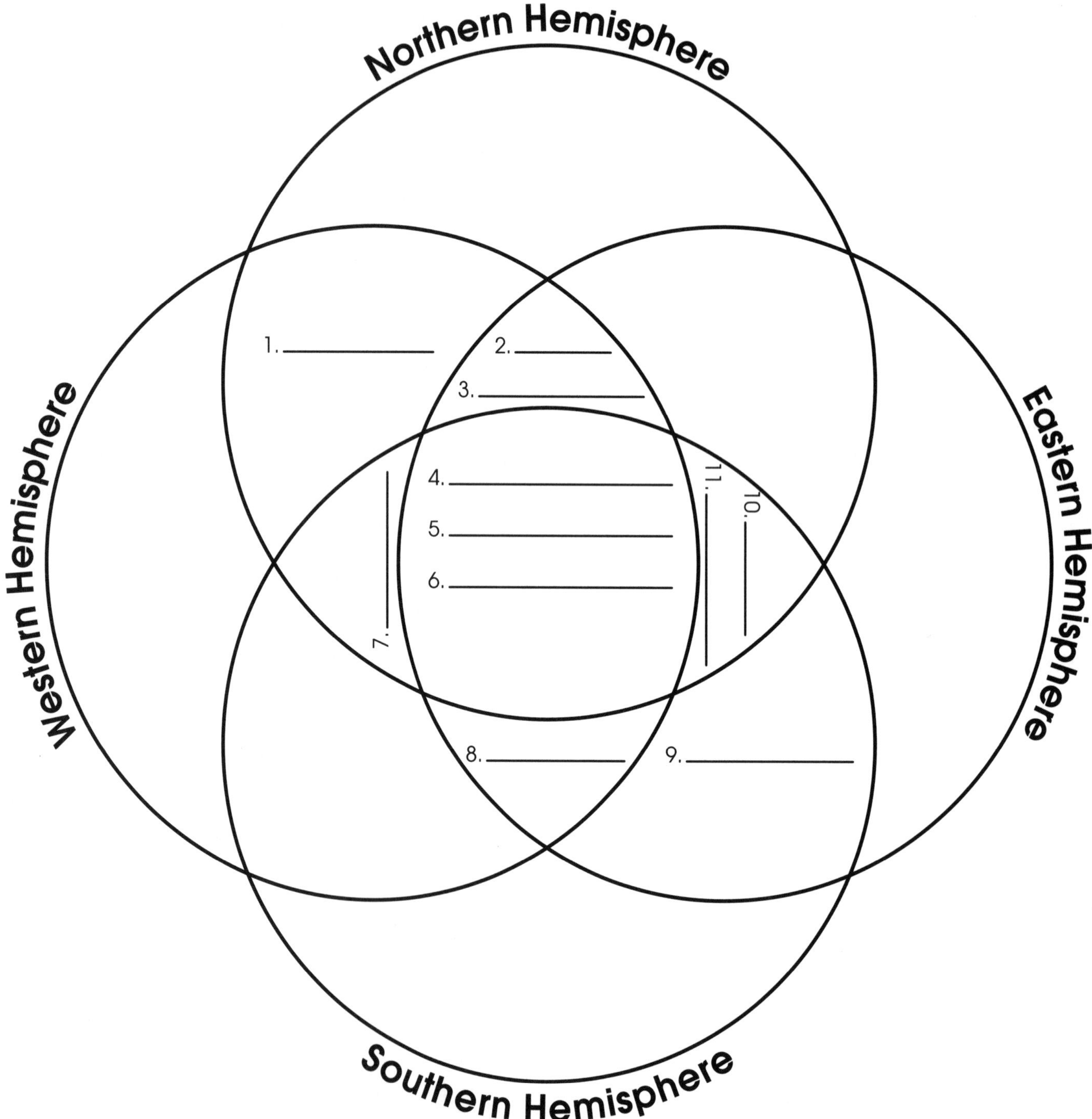

Name ____________________ National Geography Awareness Week: using a legend, critical thinking

Atlas Attractions

You've been chosen to design the new Atlas Attractions theme park. The park will be built in a wilderness, making use of all its landforms and bodies of water.

Directions: Study the map below and each of its various landforms. Next read over the list of rides that will be part of the park. Then carefully select the ride that is best suited for each landform. Write the name of the ride in the space provided.

Legend:

- = lake
- = plains
- = coastal beach
- = river
- = mountain range
- = desert
- = forest
- = valley
- = peak

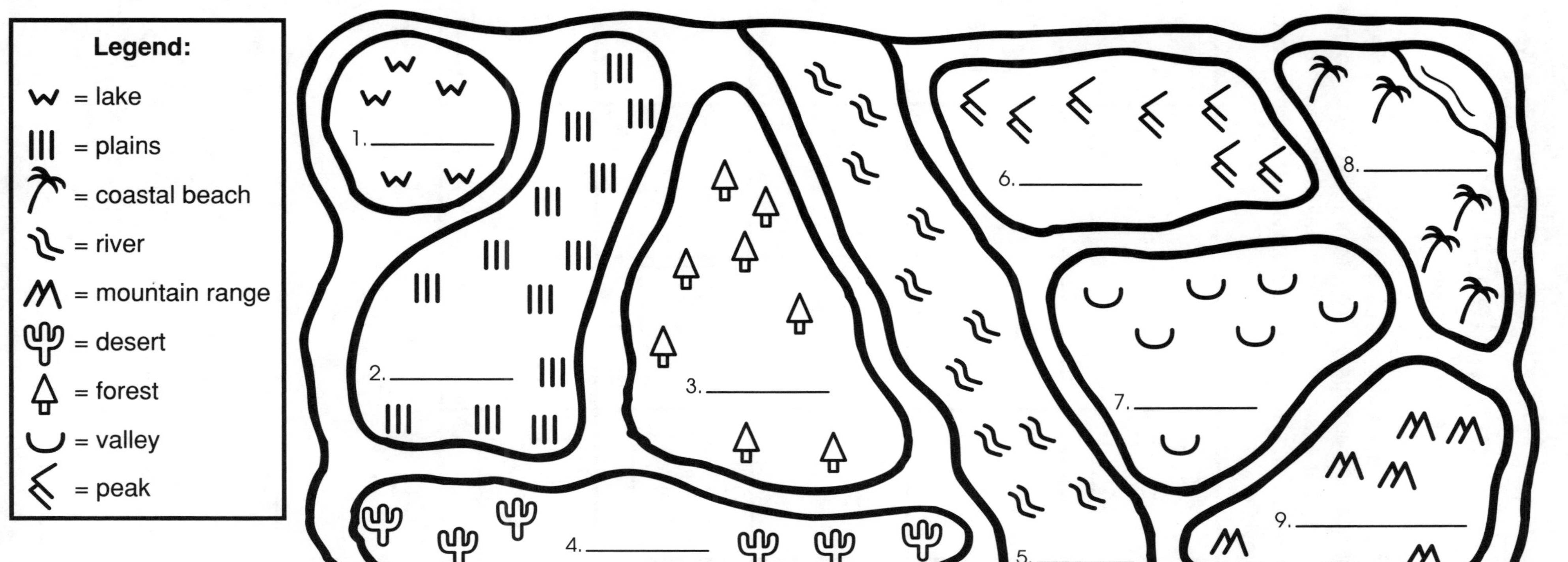

Theme Park Rides:

- Bobby's Bumper Boat Bonanza
- Simply Skateboard World
- Wanda's Winter Wonderland
- Bodine's Buffalo Stampede
- Ronnie's Raging Rapids
- Harry's Hang-Gliding Haven
- Connie's Climbing Camp
- Susie's Surf 'n' Slide
- Carmen's Camel Capers

Name ______________________________

Coordinate Chaos!

It's Daniel Deliveryboy's first day delivering newspapers, and he's having a hard time locating his customers! Help Daniel learn how to use a *coordinate system.*

A coordinate system helps you locate a place on a grid by using an *ordered pair.* The letter and number in an ordered pair are called *coordinates.* The letter tells how far to move to the right. The number tells how far up to move. For example, the Town Hall is located in grid square C–4.

Below is a grid square showing Daniel's delivery route. Write the correct coordinate pair for each address in the blank provided.

	A	B	C	D	E	F
5		Mr. Shelton	Elm Street	Alice Herndon		
4	The Richards		Town Hall Oak Drive		Mr. Ross	
3	Pine Street	Poplar Way	Spruce Lane	Cherry Lane Miss Kate Birch Lane	Cedar Drive	Mrs. Adams
2		The Helmsleys	The Barkleys Maple Road			
1		Sir Duke			Allen Hershey	

1. The Helmsleys ______________
2. Mrs. Adams ______________
3. The Richards ______________
4. The Barkleys ______________
5. Alice Herndon ______________
6. Mr. Ross ______________
7. Allen Hershey ______________
8. Mr. Shelton ______________
9. Miss Kate ______________
10. Sir Duke ______________

Name ________________________________

"A-mazing" States

Directions: Complete the maze below by connecting each state with a bordering state using a horizontal, vertical, or diagonal line. Try to complete the maze without looking at a map, but if you get stuck, pull out a United States map to get you going again.

FINISH → (Washington row)

START → (Maine row)

Washington	Oregon	California	Arizona	Utah	New Mexico
Maine	New Hampshire	Nevada	Idaho	Colorado	Texas
Connecticut	Vermont	Montana	Wyoming	Kansas	Oklahoma
New York	Rhode Island	Massachusetts	Nebraska	Iowa	South Dakota
Maryland	New Jersey	Pennsylvania	Alabama	Minnesota	North Dakota
Virginia	Delaware	Florida	Mississippi	Louisiana	Wisconsin
Kentucky	West Virginia	Georgia	Arkansas	Missouri	Michigan
Tennessee	North Carolina	South Carolina	Illinois	Indiana	Ohio

A Hodgepodge Of Map Skills

Create your own unique hodgepodge map by selecting *two* of the map options from the list below. Design appropriate map symbols; then add them to the key at the bottom of the page.

Map Options:

- On the map, mark the location of the home cities of all the major-league baseball teams and professional football teams.
- Using the weather map from a local newspaper, find the ten cities with the highest and lowest temperatures in the United States for that day. Mark them on your map.
- Research the birthplaces of ten famous people. Mark them on the map.
- List ten of your favorite movies or books and their settings. Mark the city or state of each setting on the map.

Map Key

PEANUT BUTTER LOVERS' MONTH

November has been set aside as Peanut Butter Lovers' Month to celebrate America's favorite food and number one sandwich. Your students will naturally enjoy the following peanutty activities and reproducibles!

Peanuts On Parade

Your students will go nuts over the following art and writing activity. First inform students that this member of the pea family is not a nut at all. Further explain that peanuts are also known as *goobers, groundnuts, arachides, mani,* or *pinders.* Let your students get more familiar with peanuts by having each student examine a whole, unshelled peanut. Show the student how to gently break the unshelled peanut open so that there are two equal halves. Supply each student with a variety of craft supplies, glue, and one 9" x 12" sheet of oaktag. Instruct each student to use the craft supplies to turn his peanut shells into unique peanut characters with arms, legs, faces, etc. Have the student glue his finished characters onto the sheet of oaktag. Then have each student write a story about his peanut characters, naming them and telling about their lives and adventures. Have each student share his characters and story with his classmates. Display the finished creations on a bulletin board for all to enjoy. *(**IMPORTANT NOTE:** Some students may be allergic to peanuts. Be sure to check with the school nurse before allowing students to munch.)*

Peanut-Butter Possibilities

Here's a quick, fun team game that will get your students to use their divergent thinking skills as well as their listening skills. Divide the class into teams of four. Post a large piece of chart paper labeled "Peanut-Butter Possibilities" on the chalkboard. Instruct each team to brainstorm a list of uses for peanut butter (factual and creative) and record the list on a sheet of notebook paper. Next have one member from each team record one of its listed uses on the posted sheet of chart paper. Each team is awarded one point for each new use listed. Uses cannot be repeated. If a team repeats an idea that is already on the chart, the team loses a turn and is not awarded a point. Have groups meet periodically throughout November to brainstorm more uses for peanut butter. At the end of the month, award the team with the most points some type of peanut-buttery treat.

Peanut-Butter Sandwich Hall Of Fame

Peanut butter and pickles? Peanut butter and bananas? Peanut butter and sardines? The number of peanut-butter sandwich combinations is endless, and most everyone probably has a favorite or unique way to make a peanut-butter sandwich. Have each student write a how-to paragraph describing how she makes her favorite peanut-butter sandwich. Trim a sheet of poster board to look like a piece of bread and title it "Peanut-Butter Sandwich Hall of Fame." As each student presents her speech, enter her name and her sandwich's name into the Hall of Fame. Combine the how-to paragraphs into a class recipe book titled "Our Peanut-Butter Sandwich Hall of Fame."

Names ______________________________

The Scoop On Peanut Butter

Your team is part of a consumer awareness group evaluating different brands of peanut butter. Your job is to collect data on different brands of peanut butter. Complete the chart; then analyze the data and be ready to report your findings to your classmates.

Nutrition Facts **Based on a serving size of 2 Tablespoons (Tbsp) or (32g)**				
Brands	1. ______	2. ______	3. ______	4. ______
Calories				
Calories From Fat				
Total Fat				
Cholesterol				
Sodium				
Carbohydrate				
Dietary Fiber				
Sugars				
Protein				
Vitamin A				
Vitamin C				
Calcium				
Iron				
Niacin				

Taste-Test Poll **Rating Scale: 1 = poor, 2 = good, 3 = great**				
Group Member	Brand #1 ______	Brand #2 ______	Brand #3 ______	Brand #4 ______
1				
2				
3				
4				
5				

Cost Comparison				
Price	Brand #1 $ ______	Brand #2 $ ______	Brand #3 $ ______	Brand #4 $ ______

Conclusions:

1. Which brand(s) would you recommend based on nutrition facts? ______________
2. Which brand(s) would you recommend based on taste? ______________
3. Which brand(s) would you recommend based on cost? ______________

Note To The Teacher: Divide students into small groups. Give each group one copy of this page; four small same-sized jars of peanut butter, each a different brand and labeled with its price; and one spoon for each group member.

Names ____

Make Pete's Peanuts Number One

Hi! I'm Pete, the owner and president of Pete's Peanuts. I want my company to be the number one seller of peanut butter in the country. That's why I hired you. I want your design team to invent a new peanut-butter product that everyone will love. Use the planning sheet below to name, describe, and design your new product. Then use your completed planning sheet to develop an advertising campaign poster that will make everyone in the country want to run out and buy this great new product! Be clever! Be imaginative! Remember, I'm counting on you to make Pete's Peanuts number one!

PETE'S PEANUTS

DESIGN PLANS

Product Planning Team Members

Product Description: ____

____

____

____

____

Package Design

Poster Layout

Commercial Ideas: ____

____

____

Note To The Teacher: Divide students into small cooperative teams. Provide each team with one copy of this page, one sheet of poster board, and markers.

 Name ______________________________

Where Do Those Peanuts Grow?

Peanuts grow best with a lot of sunshine and a moderate amount of rainfall (about 7–13 days of rain per month). They also need warm temperatures (approximately 54°F–94°F) and a frost-free (above 32°F) growing period of four or five months.

Directions: For each month in the chart below, the first column tells the daily average high temperature and the daily average low temperature. The second column tells the number of days that month that the state had at least .01 inches of rain. Use the information at the top of the page and the data in the chart below to determine which of the states below are peanut-growing states.

	JAN.		FEB.		MAR.		APR.		MAY		JUNE		JULY		AUG.		SEPT.		OCT.		NOV.		DEC.	
STATE	HI LO	Rain Days	HI LO	Rain Days	HI LO	Rain Days	HI LO	Rain Days	HI LO	Rain Days	HI LO	Rain Days	HI LO	Rain Days	HI LO	Rain Days	HI LO	Rain Days	HI LO	Rain Days	HI LO	Rain Days	HI LO	Rain Days
Georgia	51 33	11	55 36	10	61 41	12	71 51	9	79 59	9	85 67	10	87 69	12	86 69	9	81 63	7	73 52	6	62 41	8	53 34	10
Virginia	49 32	10	50 33	10	57 39	11	68 48	10	76 57	10	84 66	9	87 70	11	85 69	11	80 64	8	70 53	8	61 43	8	51 34	9
Arizona	65 38	3	69 41	4	75 45	3	84 52	2	93 60	1	102 68	1	105 78	5	102 76	4	98 69	3	88 57	3	75 45	2	66 39	2
Alabama	54 34	11	57 36	11	65 42	11	75 51	9	83 58	9	88 66	10	90 70	13	90 69	10	85 63	8	76 51	6	64 40	9	56 35	11
North Carolina	57 36	11	59 38	10	65 44	10	74 52	8	81 61	9	87 68	10	89 72	13	88 71	13	84 66	9	75 55	7	67 44	7	58 37	9
Nevada	56 33	3	61 37	2	68 42	3	78 50	2	88 59	1	97 67	1	104 75	3	102 73	3	95 65	2	81 53	2	66 41	2	57 34	2
Oregon	44 33	19	50 36	16	54 37	17	60 41	14	67 46	12	72 52	9	79 55	4	78 55	5	74 51	7	63 45	13	52 39	17	46 35	19
Texas	63 42	11	66 45	6	72 50	10	79 59	7	86 66	9	91 71	8	94 73	10	94 72	10	90 68	10	84 58	8	73 49	8	66 43	9

Organize:

1. With a yellow marker, highlight the facts in the paragraph at the top of the page that are important for growing peanuts.
2. With a light blue marker, highlight all the rainfall blocks that show a moderate amount of rainfall between _____–_____ days a month.
3. With a yellow marker, highlight all the HI temperatures that show warm temperatures between _____°F–_____°F.
4. With a pink marker, highlight all the LO temperatures that are frost-free, above _____°F.

Analyze:

1. With your pencil, go across each state's row and circle any month that has all three facts highlighted—HI, LO, and Rain Days.
2. Based on the information in the chart above, name five states that would be good for growing peanuts: ______________________, ______________________, ______________________, ______________________, ______________________
3. On the back of this paper, name the states that are not peanut-growing states and explain why they might not be peanut-growing states based on the data.
4. Be prepared to defend your answers with facts.

Note To The Teacher: Students will need light-colored markers. Discuss student results. Encourage students to defend their thinking with facts.

Thanksgiving

Thanksgiving Day, celebrated on the fourth Thursday in November, is a time to celebrate blessings and express thanks. Many current Thanksgiving traditions began when the Pilgrims of Plymouth Colony gave thanks for their first year's good harvest in 1621. In 1863 Abraham Lincoln proclaimed Thanksgiving a national celebration.

Nov. 30

Dec. 1

1. I'm thankful that Ashlyn is feeling better and is back at school today.
2. I'm thankful that Anwar shared his candy bar with me!
3. I'm thankful I spent extra time studying for the test today.
4. I'm thankful my dad is back from his business trip.
5. I'm thankful that I found my lost jacket during lunch.

Attitudes Of Gratitude

Thanksgiving is a time to focus on things for which we are thankful. What better time to begin a yearlong project to cultivate attitudes of gratitude in your classroom? Set aside a few minutes of class time each day for each student to write in a gratitude journal. Direct each student to write at least one thing a day for which he is thankful. Have student volunteers share entries aloud or have students swap journals and read each other's entries. Encourage students to share messages of gratitude toward fellow classmates. End every day on a thankful note and you'll all enjoy the bounty of better attitudes!

Thank you for helping me with my math when I don't understand.
—Katie

Thanks-A-Lot Napkin-Ring Notes

Make everyone feel appreciated at your classroom Thanksgiving meal with this simple art project. To begin the project, place each student's name in a hat; then have each student draw another student's name from the hat. Next provide each student with one fancy paper dinner napkin, one 6 1/2" x 1 1/2" strip of autumn-colored construction paper, scissors, a black marker, and crayons or Thanksgiving stickers. Instruct the student to cut a slit halfway through each end of her strip as shown. On one side of the strip, have the student write her classmate's name with a marker. Then have the student decorate around the name with Thanksgiving art or stickers. On the other side of the strip, direct the student to write a secret thank-you message to her classmate. Have the student form the napkin ring by rolling the strip and sliding the two slits together as shown. Have the student roll the napkin and insert it into the ring. Encourage the student to repeat the activity at home, making a napkin ring for every member of the family.

Name ______________________________

Seven Steps To Success

Many years ago, a magazine editor named Sarah Hale worked to have Thanksgiving become an annual national holiday. For more than 20 years, she wrote letters to government officials asking that a national day of thanksgiving be established. Finally, in 1863, President Abraham Lincoln proclaimed the fourth Thursday in November as Thanksgiving Day. Sarah Hale stuck with it, doing whatever it took for as long as needed to accomplish her goal. Use the goal planner below to follow in her footsteps to success!

______________________________ **'s Goal Planner**
(Student's Name)

STEP 1: Choose a goal.
Is there a habit you'd like to break or establish? Is there a problem in your community you'd like to help solve? Do you have a grade or skill you'd like to improve? Select a goal and list it below.

My goal is... ______________________________

____

STEP 2: Why do I want to achieve this goal?

Reason 1— ______________________________

____

Reason 2 — ______________________________

____

STEP 3: Things I need to do
List the things you need to do in order to achieve your goal.

1. ______________________________
2. ______________________________
3. ______________________________
4. ______________________________
5. ______________________________
6. ______________________________
7. ______________________________
8. ______________________________
9. ______________________________
10. ______________________________

STEP 4: Troubleshooting
Look over your list in Step 3. Put a * beside each number that you feel may be difficult to accomplish.

STEP 5: Make a plan.
For each number in Step 3 that you marked with a *, write a brief plan of how you might deal with this problem. Use the back of this sheet if you need more room.

____

____

____

____

____

STEP 6: Support people
Make a list of support people you can count on to help you achieve your goal.

______________ ______________

______________ ______________

______________ ______________

STEP 7: Evaluate your progress.
Make a list of the signs of success you expect to see and when you expect to see them as you strive to meet your goal.

____

____

____

____

Pilgrimage To The Next New World

Pretend you are going on a pilgrimage to the *next* new world, a planet far away from Earth. Like the original pilgrims, you don't quite know what you'll find there, but you're willing and even eager to go. You are allowed to take with you one cargo container the size of a shoebox. What will you take?

Directions: Work with your group members to complete each activity below. Beginning with Step 10, color each starburst as you complete the activity.

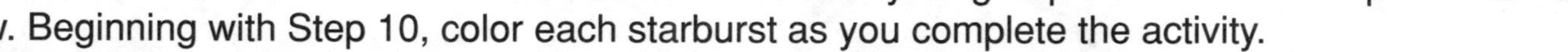

10 Brainstorm a list of necessities—things you literally cannot live without.

____

____

____

____

____

____

____

____

____

____

____

____

9 Have each member in your group share his or her list of items with the rest of the group. Afterwards, add to or delete any items from your list.

8 As a group, decide whether basic supplies like soap and toothpaste will be shared or whether each passenger will be responsible for his or her own. If your group decides to share items, list them in the space below. Beside each item, write the name of each group member responsible for packing that item.

____

____

____

____

7 Brainstorm a list of other personal items you would like to bring.

____

____

____

____

____

____

____

6 Your teacher will give your group one cargo container (a shoebox) to inspect. Remember that each traveler will get to take one cargo container. Decide which items on your lists will not fit in a container and cross them off your lists.

5 From the remaining items on the lists, circle those that are most important.

4 Using the list of circled items, make a new list on another sheet of paper of the belongings that will fit into your cargo container.

3 If not everything you want to take will fit, brainstorm for ways to eliminate items.

2 Make one last effort to take all of your most prized possessions with you. Can you borrow space from a shipmate who has extra room? Can you agree to share certain items? Can you think of other solutions? Write your solutions on the back of this page.

1 Revise your list of the items you've chosen; then put a * beside the items that are most important to you.

0 Share your list with your group members. Then prepare for…

BLASTOFF!

Note To The Teacher: Divide the class into groups of four. Provide each student with one copy of this page. Provide each group with an empty shoebox and lid to serve as a sample cargo container.

Name ______________________________

Giving Thanks Around The World

Many cultures have Thanksgiving celebrations, although they may not occur at the same time of year or include the same traditions. Use reference materials to research the Thanksgiving tradition of another culture. You may find that it is called a harvest celebration instead. Then use the diagram below to compare your Thanksgiving traditions with those of the culture you researched. Write information about *your* Thanksgiving celebration in the bottom shape near the turkey. Write the information you found about another culture's Thanksgiving celebration in the top shape, adding appropriate decorations. In the space where the two shapes overlap, write some ways the two celebrations are alike.

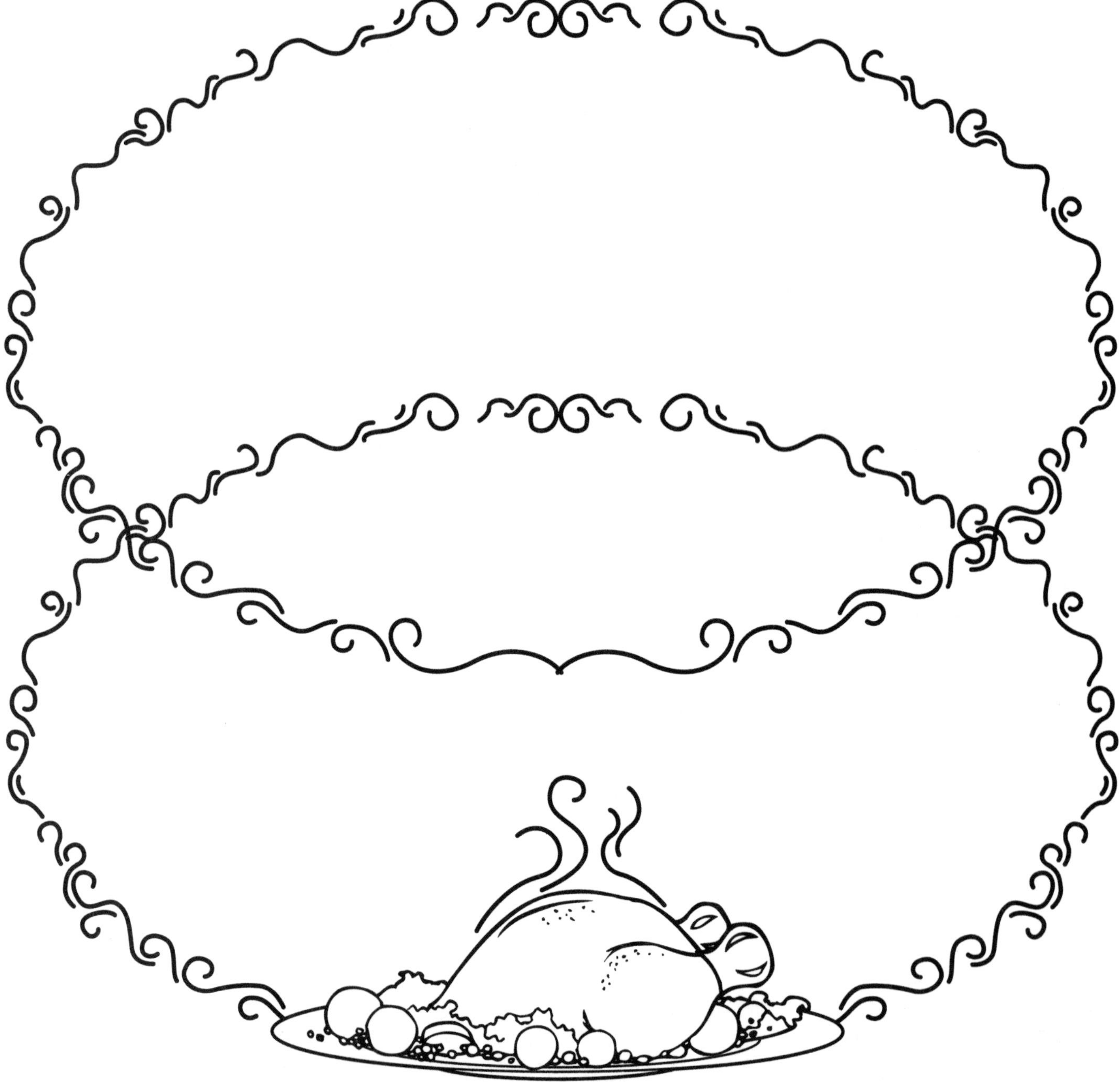

Bonus Box: On the back of this page, write a paragraph explaining the similarities between the two Thanksgiving traditions.

Note To The Teacher: Bind the completed diagrams in a booklet titled "Giving Thanks Around The World"; then display it for viewing during the holiday season.

Name ______________________________ Thanksgiving: problem solving

Places, Please!

The students at Highland School are making placemats for a special Thanksgiving lunch to be served in the cafeteria. Use the clues to find each person's place at the table. Write each person's name on the appropriate placemat on each table.

Clues:

1. Kellie will sit at the right end of the table.
2. Francesca will sit opposite Kellie.
3. Henry will sit opposite Ross.
4. Chad will sit next to Kellie, on her left.
5. Ross will sit next to Francesca, on her left.
6. Riley will sit next to Ross.

Left

Right

Clues:

1. Adrienne will sit next to Beau, on his right.
2. Amber will sit opposite Kyrsten.
3. Kyrsten will sit to the left of Michiko.
4. Michiko will sit at the left end of the table.
5. Garret will sit opposite Adrienne.
6. Beau will sit opposite Michiko.

Left

Right

Name ______________________________

Add Up The Answer

Do you know which side of a turkey has the most feathers? Find the sums; then use the key to solve the riddle by matching each letter to its answer below each blank. The first one is done for you.

1. 1,423 + 1,219 = 2,642 **I**
2. 1,692 + 1,452 = ____ **O**
3. 1,993 + 1,998 = ____ **C**
4. 1,361 + 260 = ____
5. 5,692 + 3,856 = ____ **U**
6. 6,354 + 1,243 = ____ **T**
7. 1,215 + 2,695 = ____ **R**
8. 3,564 + 758 = ____ **E**
9. 6,784 + 2,137 = ____ **F**
10. 4,316 + 1,309 = ____ **S**
11. 6,244 + 2,296 = ____ **H**
12. 8,161 + 1,219 = ____ **D**

Which side of a turkey has the most feathers?

___ ___ ___
7,597 8,540 4,322

___ ___ ___ ___ I ___ ___,
3,144 9,548 7,597 5,625 2,642 9,380 4,322

___ ___
3,144 8,921

___ ___ ___ ___ ___ ___!
3,991 3,144 9,548 3,910 5,625 4,322

Bonus Box: What does the answer to problem number 4 have to do with Thanksgiving?

LATIN AMERICA WEEK

Latin America Week, observed the last full week in November, celebrates the history and culture of Mexico, the countries in Central America and South America, and the Caribbean.

SOMETHING TO CROW ABOUT

This adaptation of the classic Latin American game *Pipis y Gallos* (The Cock Fight) will have your students strutting their stuff in no time! After introducing the Spanish color words at the right, prepare two five-inch squares of construction paper for each of the colors. Then choose two students to play the game while the others form a circle around them. Use a safety pin or tape to attach one colored square of paper to each player's back without letting the other player see the color.

To play the game: Two students face each other, arms folded in imitation of wings, in the center of the circle. At the sound of the start signal, instruct each student to try to discover the color of her opponent's paper without allowing the other player to see her own. Inform the players that touching is not allowed. The first student to call out her opponent's color in Spanish wins and gets to choose a new opponent. Continue to play until everyone has had a turn.

MEXICAN MEMORY

Help your students learn how to count from one to ten in Spanish with the following matching game. Divide students into pairs. Give each pair 20 index cards. Instruct each pair to write the Spanish name for the numbers one to ten on separate cards. Then have the pair draw a corresponding number of Latin American objects for each number on a separate card, such as two sombreros for the number two. Combine pairs into groups of four. Have each group combine and shuffle the two sets of cards into one large deck before placing them facedown on a flat surface. To play the game, have students take turns flipping over two cards at a time. A match is made when a number card and its matching illustrated card are revealed and the student correctly pronounces the number in Spanish. If the two cards do not match, then they are placed facedown again in the same places. Play continues until all matches have been made. The student with the most matches wins!

1—uno (oo-noh)
2—dos (dohs)
3—tres (trays)
4—cuatro (kwah-troh)
5—cinco (theen-koh)
6—seis (says)
7—siete (see-eh-tay)
8—ocho (oh-choh)
9—nueve (nway-bay)
10—diez (dee-ayth)

black—negro (nay-gro)
blue—azul (ah-sool)
brown—moreno (more-eh-no)
gray—gris (grees)
green—verde (bear-day)
orange—anaranjado (ah-nah-rahn-ha-do)
pink—rosa (roh-sah)
purple—morado (more-ah-do)
red—rojo (roh-ho)
white—blanco (blan-ko)
yellow—amarillo (ahm-ar-ee-yo)

Name ____

A GOLD MINE OF INFORMATION

The Spanish came to the New World in search of gold. They looked far and wide, believing the legend of El Dorado, a city of gold. Use a world map and the clues below to introduce yourself to a wealth of information about Mexico, Central America, South America, and the Caribbean. Write your answers in the blanks provided as you work your way toward Tonatiuh, the Aztec's golden king of the planets.

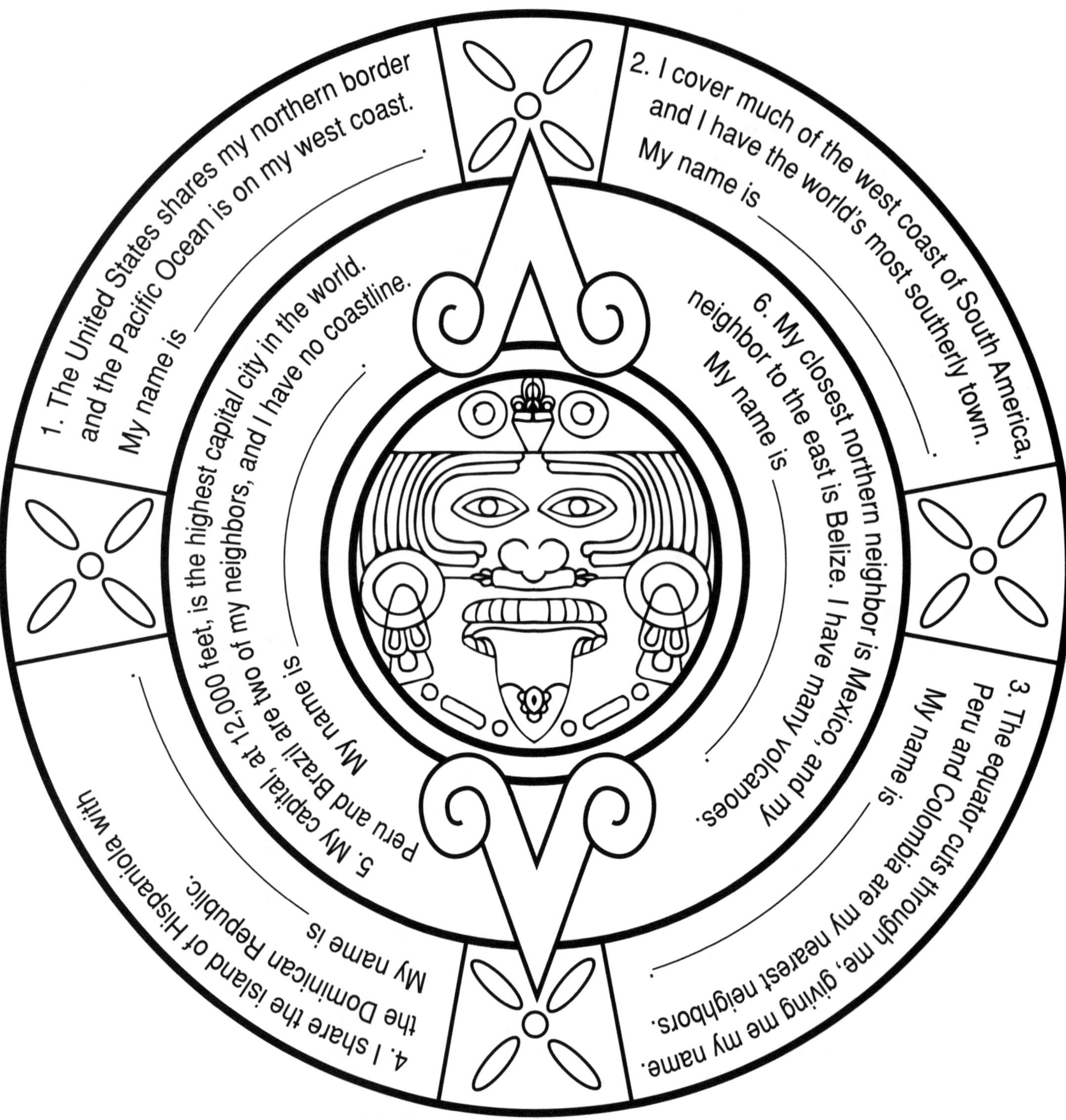

Bonus Box: Write your own clues to other Latin American countries and give them to a classmate to solve.

Name ______________________________

QUICK FACTS CODEX

The Aztecs, a powerful Indian empire in Mexico over 400 years ago, used a small foldout book called a *codex* to record information about their daily lives and history. Choose a Latin American country to research; then follow the directions below to create your own codex full of quick facts.

Materials:
two 8 1/2" x 11" sheets of white paper, two 5" x 6" pieces of poster board, tape, glue, scissors, markers or crayons

Directions:

1. Fold both sheets of paper in half lengthwise. Cut along each fold.
2. Tape the four pieces together to form one long strip as shown.

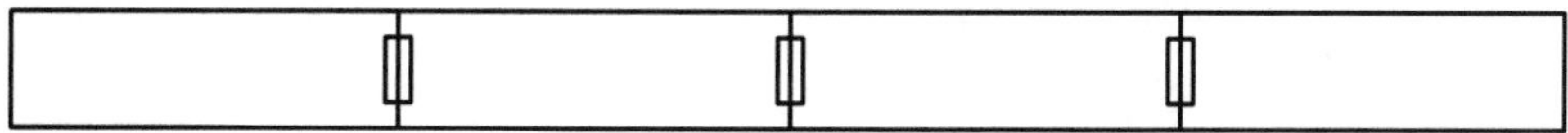

3. Fold the long strip back and forth like an accordian so that the book has eight equal parts as shown.

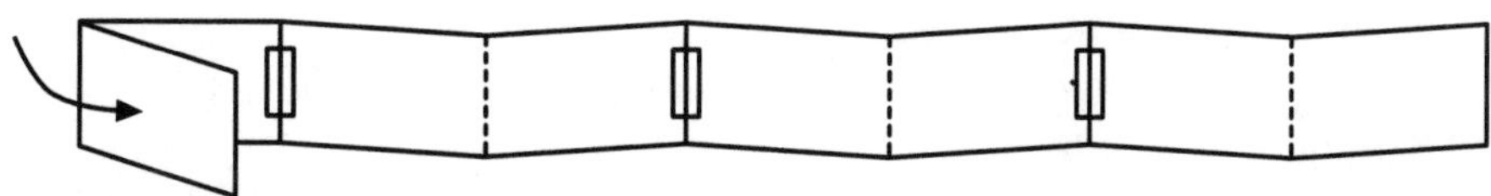

4. Glue the poster-board pieces onto the two ends of the strip to create covers.

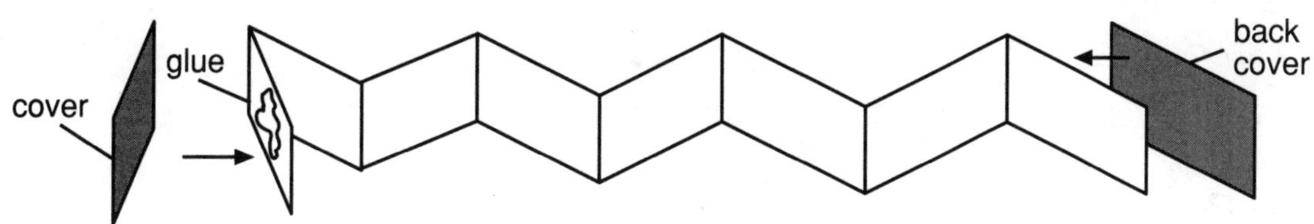

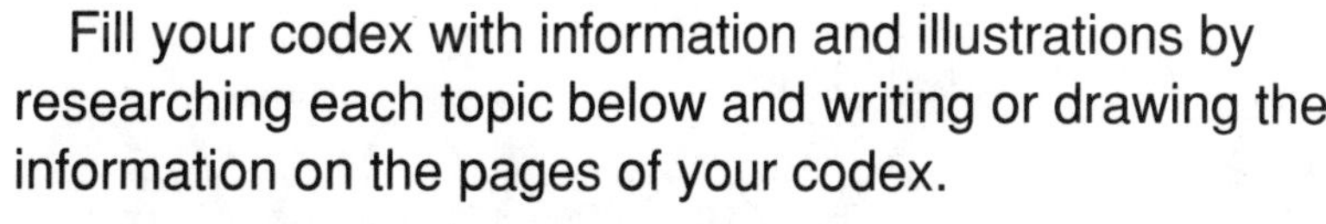

Fill your codex with information and illustrations by researching each topic below and writing or drawing the information on the pages of your codex.

Cover: Country's official name
Page 1: Official flag or seal
Page 2: Outline map of country with capital labeled
Page 3: Climate
Page 4: People
Page 5: Official language and other languages spoken
Page 6: The economy: main products and industry, currency
Page 7: Education
Page 8: Interesting facts about your country

Note To The Teacher: For information about the individual countries of Latin America, visit the Atlapedia Web site at http://www.atlapedia.com. *(Current as of 10/98)*

Name ______________________________

CALCULATOR CLIMB

While climbing a pyramid in Guatemala, Yona and her cousin Sevillio are trying to decide who is older. Since Yona says she is 13 and Sevillio says he is 18, it seems like there's not much to argue about. However, Sevillio, like many people in his part of Guatemala, figures his age using the ancient Mayan calendar, which has only 260 days. Yona measures her age by using the Gregorian calendar, the same calendar as you use, which has 365 days.

Use your calculator to settle the argument and solve each question as Yona and Sevillio climb the ancient pyramid. Write your answers in the blanks provided.

6. Which cousin is older? __________
   By how many days? __________

5. Just for the sake of argument, divide Yona's age in days by the number of days in the Mayan year.
   __________ days old ÷ 260 = Yona is __________ Mayan years old!

4. Yona says she is 13 years old. Find out how old she is in *days:*
   __________ days in the Gregorian year x __________ years old = __________ days old

3. Divide Sevillio's age in days by the number of days in the Gregorian calendar year.
   __________ days old ÷ __________ days = Sevillio is __________ Gregorian years old.

2. Sevillio says he is 18 years old. To find out how old he is by the Gregorian calendar, first find out how old he is in *days:*
   __________ days in the Mayan year x __________ years old = __________ days old

1. How many days difference is there between the two cousins' calendars?
   365 – 260 = __________

Bonus Box: On the back of this sheet, make a list of the privileges and responsibilities you expect to have when you are 18. Why do you think age makes a difference?

Name____

CRAZY ABOUT CAPITALS

Latin America is made up of Mexico, Central America, South America, and the Caribbean. Listed below are the capitals of many Latin American countries. Use a map or an atlas to help you choose the country from the word bank that matches each capital. Write the circled letters in the corresponding numbered blanks at the bottom of the page to complete the sentence that reveals what many Latin American adults and children are *crazy* about! The first one has been done for you.

Capitals:

1. Buenos Aires A r (g)[1] e n t i n a
2. Belmopan __ __ __ __ __ (__)[14]
3. Santiago (__)[12] __ __ __ __
4. Bogota __ __ __ __ __ __ __ (__)[2]
5. Quito (__)[4] __ __ __ __ __ __
6. Havana __ (__)[5] __ __
7. Mexico City __ __ __ __ (__)[13] __
8. Caracas __ __ __ __ __ __ __ (__)[9] __
9. Panama City __ __ __ __ (__)[3] __
10. San José __ (__)[8] __ (__)[6] __ __ __ __ __
11. Brasilia (__)[7] __ __ __ __ __
12. La Paz __ (__)[11] __ __ __ __ __
13. Nassau __ __ __ __ __ __ (__)[10]
14. Managua __ __ __ __ (__)[15] __ __ __ __

We love the Spanish g(1) __(2) __(3) __(4) of f __(5) __(6) __(7) __(8) __(9), which is also known as __(10) __(11) __(12) __(13) __(14) __(15).

Bonus Box: Make a list of the Latin American countries and capitals not found on the list above. Then write your own riddle about Latin American life for a classmate to solve.

Name ______________________________

CONQUER CARTOGRAPHY

Before setting off to conquer the New World, Christopher Columbus was a *cartographer,* or mapmaker, for Portugal. One kind of map cartographers make shows mountains, valleys, plains, oceans, rivers, and lakes. This kind of map is called a *physical map.* Use an atlas and the key below to help you make a physical map of South America and Central America.

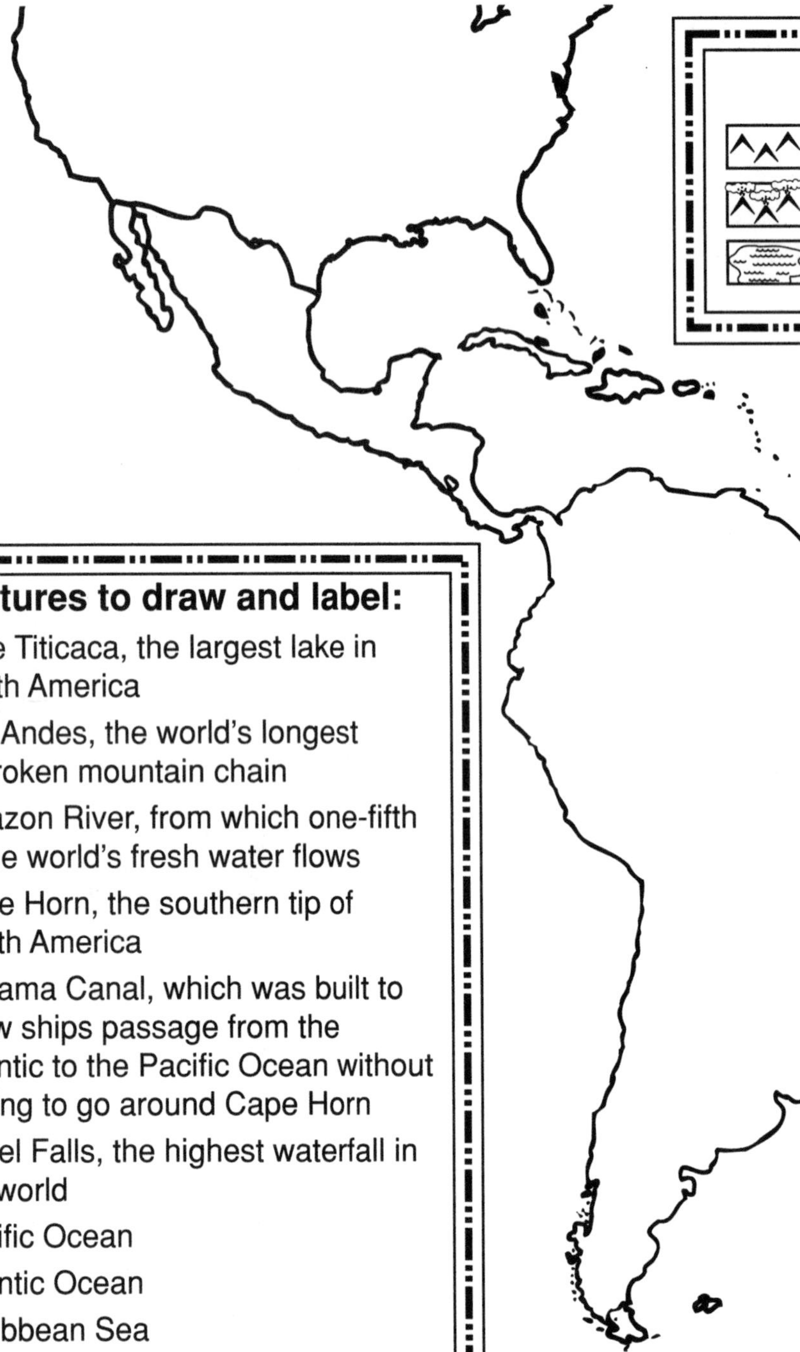

KEY:

- mountains—brown
- volcano—red
- bodies of water—blue

Features to draw and label:

- Lake Titicaca, the largest lake in South America
- The Andes, the world's longest unbroken mountain chain
- Amazon River, from which one-fifth of the world's fresh water flows
- Cape Horn, the southern tip of South America
- Panama Canal, which was built to allow ships passage from the Atlantic to the Pacific Ocean without having to go around Cape Horn
- Angel Falls, the highest waterfall in the world
- Pacific Ocean
- Atlantic Ocean
- Caribbean Sea
- Cotopaxi, one of the world's tallest active volcanoes

Bonus Box: Use a map to find the location of the Amazon rain forest. Then use a green crayon to mark the rain forest on the map above. List some of the unique birds, insects, plants, and animals that call this rain forest home.

Name ______________________________ Latin America Week: research, point of view

BOTH SIDES OF THE COIN

Every coin has two sides, and most issues do, too. Select one of the explorers listed below. Research to find out what he discovered and accomplished for his country. Record your findings on the appropriate coin below. Then research to find the effects the explorer's accomplishments had on the native peoples of the discovered areas. Record these findings on the other coin.

Explorers:

- Christopher Columbus
- Amerigo Vespucci
- Hernán Cortés
- Francisco Pizarro
- Pedro Álvares Cabral
- Pedro de Alvarado
- Francisco de Orellana
- Hernando De Soto
- Juan Ponce de Léon
- Juan Díaz de Solís
- Vasco Nuñez de Balboa
- Ferdinand Magellan
- Alonso de Ojeda
- Vicente Yáñez Pinzón

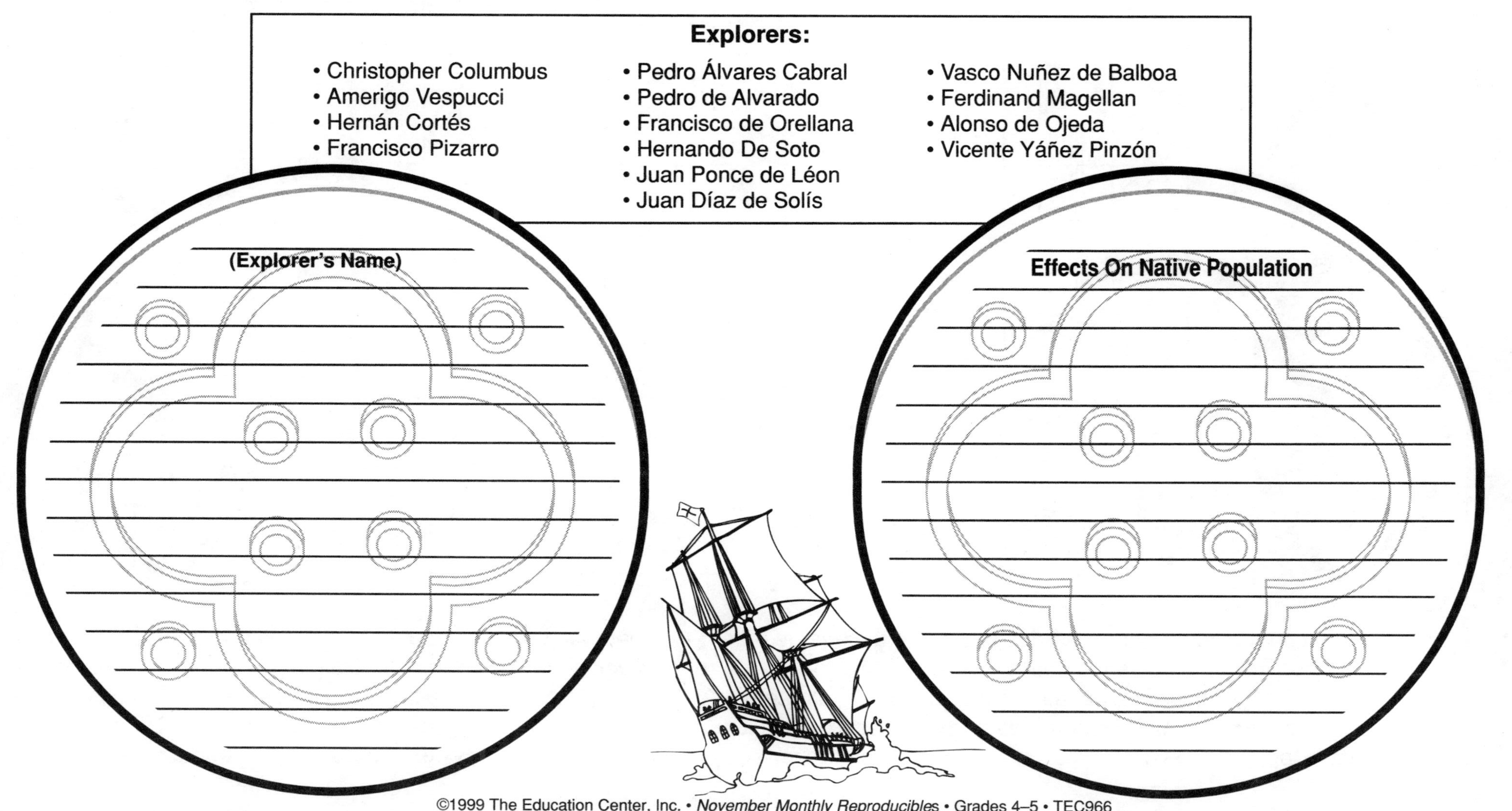

Note To The Teacher: Have each student lightly color both coins gold, then cut out each coin and glue them back-to-back. Attach a length of yarn to the top of each two-sided coin and hang the coins from the ceiling so both sides are shown.

EVERY DOT COUNTS

The Aztec Empire, which peaked around 1500 under the rule of Montezuma II, was a complex culture. The Aztecs developed their own writing, religion, and unique numbering system. Unlike our system, which is based on 10, their numbering system was based on 20 and required the use of dots and flags. Using the Aztec system, the ordered pair (20, 5) would look like the following (⚑, ...)

Fortunately, our way of writing numbers is much easier to read, write, and plot! Plot the following pairs on the graph below. Mark each point on the grid; then connect each dot in the same order to re-create an ancient Aztec design. Remember, every dot counts!

1. (4, 6)	6. (15, 8)	11. (20, 5)	16. (9, 3)
2. (6, 6)	7. (15, 7)	12. (18, 5)	17. (9, 4)
3. (6, 7)	8. (18, 7)	13. (18, 4)	18. (6, 4)
4. (9, 7)	9. (18, 6)	14. (15, 4)	19. (6, 5)
5. (9, 8)	10. (20, 6)	15. (15, 3)	20. (4, 5)

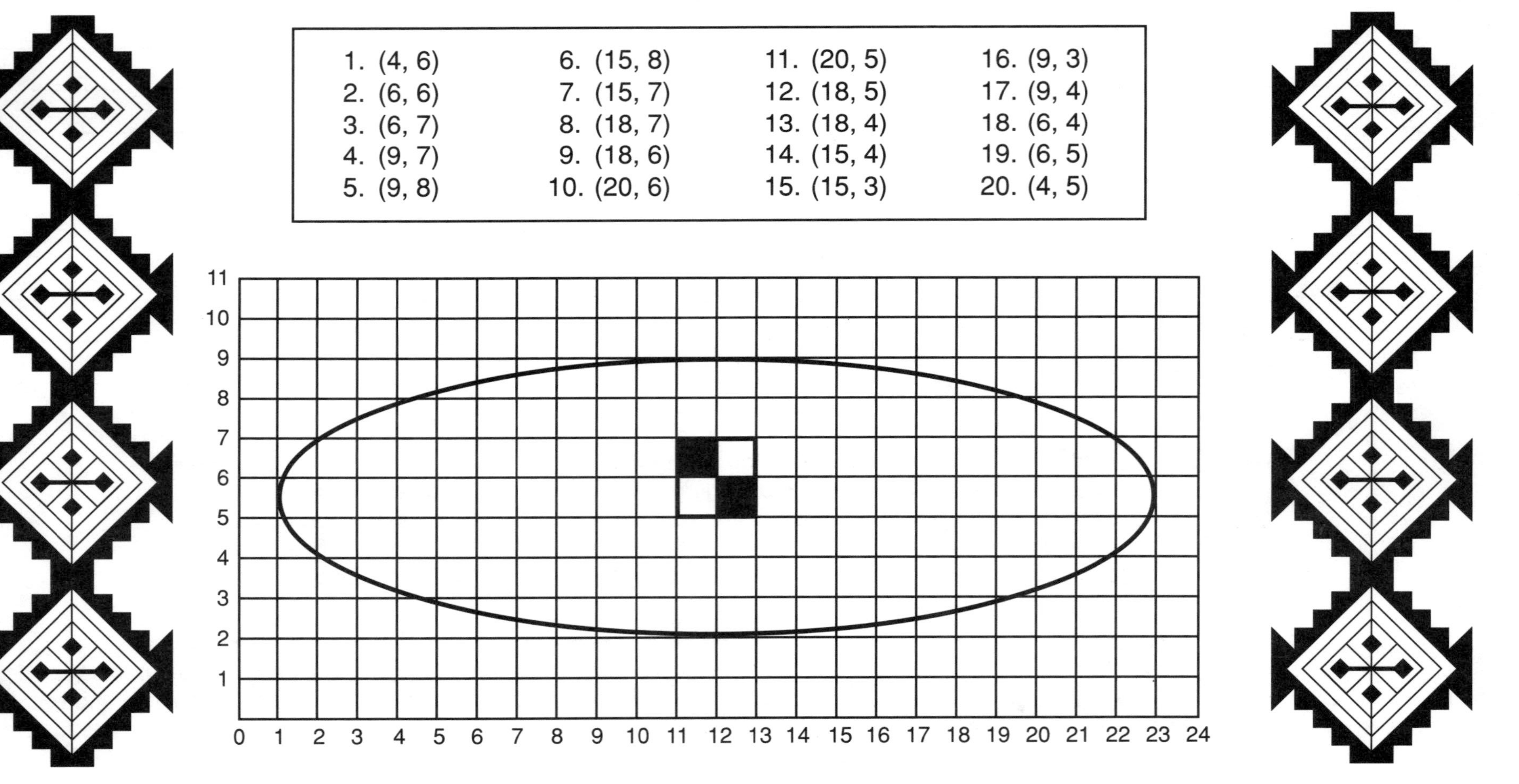

Answer Keys

Page 6
1. e
2. f
3. a
4. b
5. h
6. c
7. d
8. j
9. g
10. i

Answer to question: *nom de plume*

Page 13
1. 3.3 m x 9.5 m
2. 4.5 m x 1.5 m
3. 8.5 m

Page 14
1. b
2. a
3. b
4. c
5. a
6. c
7. c
8. c
9. b
10. b

Bonus Box answer: The B–2 (Stealth) Bomber. It is very difficult to detect on radar.

Page 16
1. about 250 miles
2. 300
3. about 850 miles
4. 350
5. about 350 miles
6. about 550 miles
7. about 1400 miles

Page 20
1. E
2. C
3. H
4. A
5. F
6. D
7. I
8. G
9. B
10. J

Bonus Box answer: When the person in charge is absent, people will usually take advantage of the freedom and do as they please.

Page 22
1. manul
2. tiger
3. lynx
4. leopard
5. ocelot
6. Manx
7. lion
8. caracal
9. Maine coon cat
10. jaguar
11. cougar
12. serval

Page 25

Page 26
1. white
2. elbow
3. Navy
4. August
5. liquid
6. United States
7. Donut who?
8. century
9. 32
10. east
11. lunch
12. foot
13. tac
14. aunt
15. condensation
16. pint
17. during
18. drop
19. look
20. elevator

Page 32
1. California (54), New York (33), Texas (32), Florida (25)
2. 144 total votes
3. 270 – 144 = 126
4. Answers will vary, but each should include North Dakota with 3 electoral votes. One possible answer: a combination of North Carolina (14), Virginia (13), Washington (11), Minnesota (10), Illinois (22), Arizona (8), Tennessee (11), Missouri (11), Pennsylvania (23), and North Dakota (3) equals the needed 126 votes.

Bonus Box answer: Yes, it is possible. The last time this happened was in 1888. President Grover Cleveland received the most popular votes; however, Benjamin Harrison was elected president because he won states that were larger and held more electoral votes.

Page 36
1. addition, 1921
2. subtraction, 63
3. addition, 1978
4. addition, 1954
5. addition, 1938
6. subtraction, 21

Order in timeline: 1, 5, 6, 4, 3, 2
1. World War I ended with a cease-fire agreement. **(1)**
2. Armistice Day became a legal holiday in 1938. **(5)**
3. World War II began in 1939. **(6)**
4. Congress changed the name of Armistice Day to Veterans Day in 1954. **(4)**
5. In 1968, Congress temporarily changed the national celebration of Veterans Day to the fourth Monday in October. **(3)**
6. Each Veterans Day, the president honors all soldiers at a ceremony held at the Tomb of the Unknowns in Arlington National Cemetery. **(2)**

Page 38
1. Colorado, Pikes Peak
2. Arkansas, Hot Springs
3. Florida, Everglades
4. Kentucky, Mammoth Cave
5. South Dakota, Mount Rushmore
6. Oregon, Crater Lake

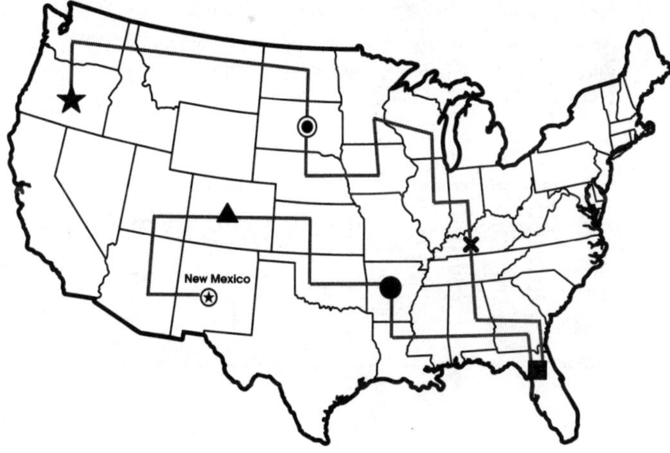

Page 40
1. North America
2. Europe
3. Arctic Ocean
4. Africa
5. Atlantic Ocean
6. Pacific Ocean
7. South America
8. Antarctica
9. Australia
10. Asia
11. Indian Ocean

Answer Keys

Page 41
1. Bobby's Bumper Boat Bonanza
2. Bodine's Buffalo Stampede
3. Wanda's Winter Wonderland
4. Carmen's Camel Capers
5. Ronnie's Raging Rapids
6. Harry's Hang-Gliding Haven
7. Simply Skateboard World
8. Susie's Surf 'n' Slide
9. Connie's Climbing Camp

Page 42
1. B–2
2. F–3
3. A–4
4. C–2
5. D–5
6. E–4
7. E–1
8. B–5
9. D–3
10. B–1

Page 43

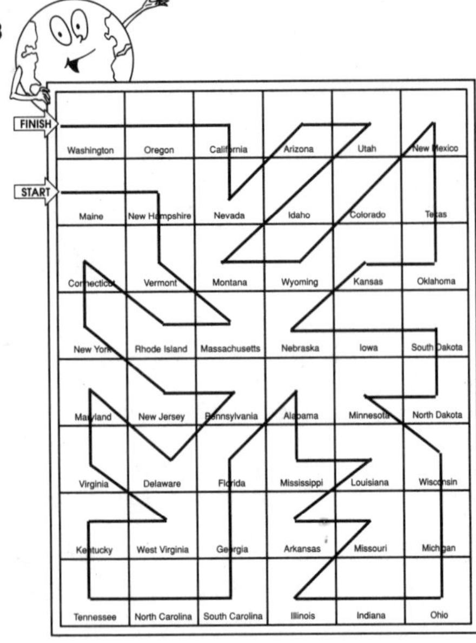

Page 48
Organize:
2. 7, 13
3. 54, 94
4. 32

Analyze:
2. Georgia, Virginia, Alabama, North Carolina, Texas
3. Arizona, Nevada, and Oregon are not peanut-growing states. Arizona and Nevada are not peanut-growing states because they do not receive enough rainfall. During most months, Oregon receives too much rainfall.

Page 53

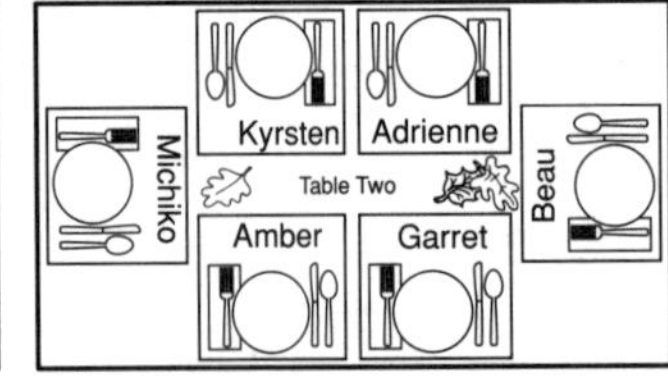

Page 54

1. 2,642	5. 9,548	9. 8,921
2. 3,144	6. 7,597	10. 5,625
3. 3,991	7. 3,910	11. 8,540
4. 1,621	8. 4,322	12. 9,380

Riddle answer: The outside, of course!
Bonus Box answer: The answer to number 4 is 1,621. In the year 1621, the first Thanksgiving celebration in New England took place at Plymouth, Massachusetts.

Page 56
1. Mexico
2. Chile
3. Ecuador
4. Haiti
5. Bolivia
6. Guatemala

Page 58
1. 105
2. 260 x 18 = 4,680
3. 4,680 ÷ 365 = 12.82
4. 365 x 13 = 4,745
5. 4,745 ÷ 260 = 18.25
6. Yona, 65 days

Page 59
1. Argentina
2. Belize
3. Chile
4. Colombia
5. Ecuador
6. Cuba
7. Mexico
8. Venezuela
9. Panama
10. Costa Rica
11. Brazil
12. Bolivia
13. Bahamas
14. Nicaragua

Answer to question: We love the Spanish **game** of **futbol,** which is also known as **soccer.**

Page 60

Page 62

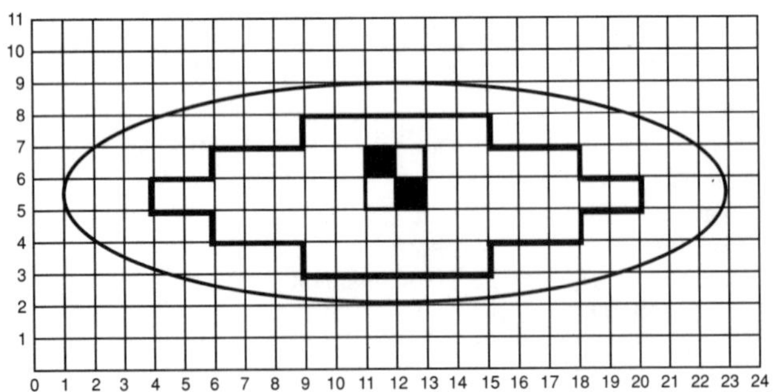